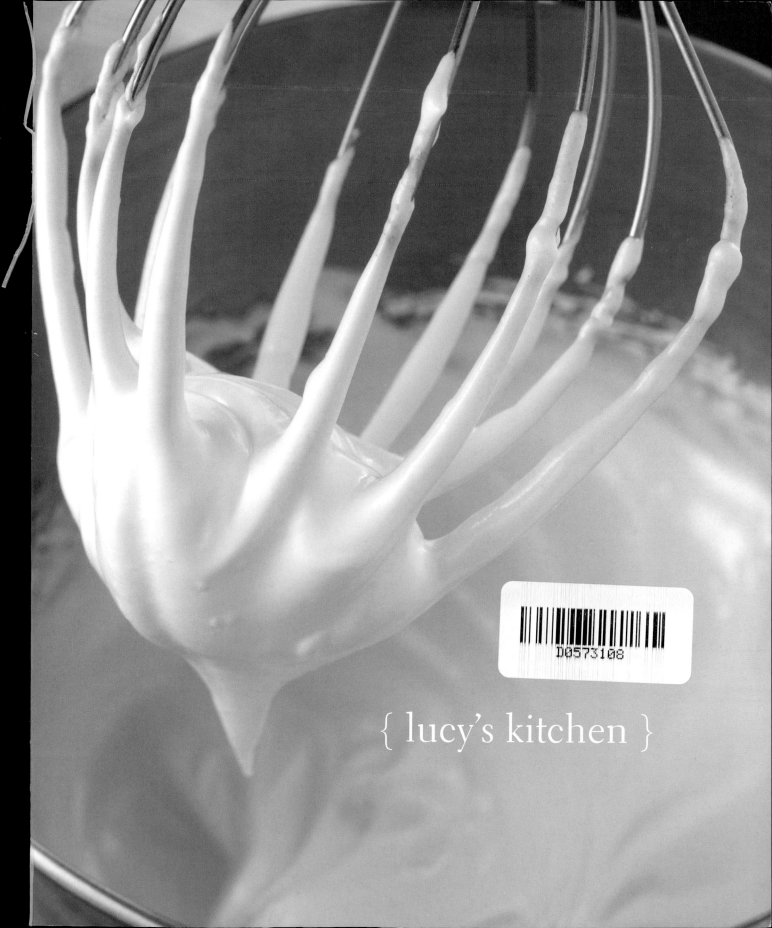

{ lucy's kitchen }

LUCY WAVERMAN

SIGNATURE RECIPES *and* CULINARY SECRETS

photography by **ROB FIOCCA**

Lucy's Kitchen

random house canada

Published in 2006 by Random House Canada, a division of
Random House of Canada Limited. Distributed in Canada
by Random House of Canada Limited.

Random House Canada and colophon are trademarks

www.randomhouse.ca

Library and Archives Canada Cataloguing in Publication

Waverman, Lucy
    Lucy's kitchen : signature recipes and culinary secrets /
Lucy Waverman ; photography by Rob Fiocca.

ISBN-13: 978-0-679-31457-8
ISBN-10: 0-679-31457-1

    1. Cookery. I. Title.
TX714.W39 2006   641.5   C2006-903005-7

Design by Kelly Hill

Printed and bound in China

10 9 8 7 6 5 4 3 2 1

to Zachary, Joshua, Liam, Noah,
Ella, Anna and Talia with love

{ contents }

My kitchen is the centre of my home—a nerve centre of warmth, good feelings and contentment. When friends and family come to visit, they invariably gravitate there for food and conversation. It isn't a big kitchen, but it is inviting, colourful and comfortable.

My kitchen has become a part of other people's lives, too, through my columns and features in the *Globe and Mail* and *Food & Drink* magazine. So I thought it would be a good idea to make my kitchen the focus of this new book. It is where I cook every day to create recipes and feed my family. It is both my work place and where my heart is.

When I was growing up, the kitchen was the pulse of the entire house—the place where I did my homework, where we all ate together, where family and close friends gathered. It took the place of today's family room. But today many kitchens are not much more than showpieces, and buying prepared foods, ordering in and eating out have taken the place of home cooking.

Now things are changing. People are coming back into the kitchen. They want to learn more about cooking and to make it a pleasurable part of their lives. I see this trend in the feedback I receive from my readers, who are asking lots of questions about cooking techniques and ingredients. They also want to eat healthier food and maintain control over what goes into their mouths. Cooking school enrolments are rising, as are television shows that include "cooking school" segments.

So, in this book, in addition to recipes, I have included short explanations of techniques and ingredients to help make cooking easier and more enjoyable. If you were never sure what it meant to fold eggs, you'll find out how in this book. Never sliced a bulb of fennel? Don't know how to clean a leek? What to do with a roast that is still underdone in the middle? These questions and many more are answered here. (At the back of this book there is a general index as well as indexes of the culinary skills and ingredients that are explained throughout the book.)

I like to create easy, foolproof recipes that have a taste twist or that provide an unusual take on a traditional favourite. I travel a lot, so there are influences from India, Asia, South America, Europe and, always, my beloved Scotland. You'll find everything from a very quick chicken curry to my latest favourites—tagliatelle with scallops infused with lemon and a cross-cuisine Malaysian beef stir-fry—to old standbys like a classic roast beef, the definitive Scottish oatmeal biscuit and the best-ever peach pie.

This book is a real reflection of my personal tastes, so you'll find lots of the foods I love best—potatoes, mushrooms, green vegetables, meat and fish. You won't find yeast breads or fussy and complicated desserts; though I was classically trained as a cook, running a cooking school, raising a family, writing books and columns and finding time for seven tiny grand-children means I do not have the time or inclination to keep four kinds of homemade stock on hand (I only make chicken stock), I'm not at all opposed to using good commercial products (storebought meringues and lemon curd), and I'm always looking for shortcuts (from cookie-crumb dessert crusts to one of my favourite tricks—the chef technique of searing the main ingredient in an ovenproof skillet and sticking the pan straight into the oven to finish the cooking).

Time is always a factor for me, whether it involves cooking, cleanup or shopping. So almost all the ingredients in my recipes can be found at your local supermarket or health food store, and I've included readily available substitutes.

To bring you even further into my kitchen, all the photographs for this book were shot there, too, using my own serving dishes and equipment. The pictures are not necessarily what we call "beauty shots" in the profession—dishes prepared in professional kitchens with the help of food stylists and prop stylists and gussied up to look beautiful without much hope that a normal cook can recreate them in the home kitchen. The pictures in this book show exactly how the food looks in the pan or on the plate. Your food can look the same.

I consider it an honour to reach so many people through my recipes, and to receive feedback from readers through my website. I hope this book will help you gain the confidence and pleasure that come with cooking and eating well.

Lucy Waverman
www.lucywaverman.com
November 2006

{ appetizers }

Warm Olives and Peppers

SERVES 4

For this little nibble, use black olives alone or try a mixture—Kalamata, sun-dried and cracked green olives are a good combination. Pit the olives if you wish and use storebought roasted or grilled peppers if you don't want to roast them yourself.

If you prepare these ahead, refrigerate the olives (they should be completely covered in oil). You can serve the olives and peppers cold, but rewarming them in the marinade in a skillet or microwave before serving enhances the flavour.

1 ½ cups mixed olives

½ cup chopped roasted red peppers

½ cup chopped roasted yellow peppers

1 cup olive oil

2 tbsp slivered garlic

5 fresh rosemary sprigs

1 tbsp grated lemon rind

1 tsp chili flakes, or to taste

Freshly ground pepper

COMBINE olives, roasted peppers, oil, garlic, rosemary, lemon rind, chili flakes and pepper in a skillet over low heat. Warm for 10 minutes, turning gently. Keep heat low enough that rosemary leaves do not sizzle.

REMOVE from heat and cool slightly. Remove olives and peppers from oil to serve.

{ olives }

The only difference between green olives and black olives is ripeness (green olives are unripe). There are many varieties, but they are all brined before being sold.

KALAMATA OLIVES • Large, purple, almond-shaped olives from Greece. They are soft but not mushy and are used in cooking and in tapenade, a savoury spread made with black olives, olive oil and garlic.

NIÇOISE OLIVES • Small black olives cured in red wine vinegar and herbs. They are superb for nibbling.

SUN-DRIED OLIVES • Sweeter than other black olives, these are easy to pit; just squeeze out the pits with your fingers.

CRACKED GREEN OLIVES • These tart and tasty olives are usually marinated in herbs and vinegar. Most green olives are pitted and stuffed.

SPANISH ARBEQUINO • Small green olives with a mild, smoky flavour. The larger, less-tasty versions are called manzanillo.

Candied Walnuts

MAKES ABOUT 1 CUP

These make a good nibble, as well as a pretty garnish for a salad. You can also make candied pecans.

2 tbsp vegetable or walnut oil	3 tbsp granulated sugar
1 cup walnut halves	

HEAT oil in small non-stick skillet over medium-low heat. Add walnuts and sauté for 1 minute.

ADD sugar and cook, stirring, until walnuts are coated with sugar and pale gold in colour, about 2 minutes. Quickly remove nuts to a parchment-lined baking sheet to cool.

Emerald Edamame Dip

MAKES ABOUT 2 CUPS

This dip is a beautiful emerald colour—very tasty and healthy. Serve it with walnut cracker bread (page 224), Belgian endive spears or other vegetables.

2 cups shelled edamame	$\frac{1}{2}$ tsp ground cumin
$\frac{1}{2}$ cup mayonnaise	$\frac{1}{2}$ tsp chili powder
$\frac{1}{2}$ cup plain yogurt	2 tbsp chopped chives
$\frac{1}{2}$ tsp lemon juice	Salt and freshly ground pepper

COMBINE edamame, mayonnaise, yogurt, lemon juice, cumin, chili powder and chives in a food processor.

SEASON with salt and pepper and process until smooth.

Savoury Cheese Stars

MAKES ABOUT 36 COOKIES

These easy savoury cookies have a superb taste and can be served on their own or topped with a little cranberry or fig relish. I have also used them as the base for sliced prosciutto and smoked turkey canapés. Use a well-flavoured old Cheddar cheese or, for a different flavour, substitute any other hard grating cheese and/or add a teaspoon of chopped fresh sage or thyme to the dough. The toppings are optional but good.

1 1/4 cups all-purpose flour
1 tsp dry mustard
1 tsp salt
1/4 tsp cayenne
1/2 cup butter, cubed
2 cups grated Cheddar cheese
1/2 cup grated Parmesan cheese
1 egg

Toppings
Chopped nuts, coarsely cracked peppercorns or coriander seeds, or chopped fennel seeds

PREHEAT oven to 375 F.

COMBINE flour, mustard, salt and cayenne in a food processor.

ADD butter, Cheddar and Parmesan and pulse just until dough comes together.

TRANSFER dough to a lightly floured board and knead a few times. Divide into four pieces.

ROLL out each piece of dough until about 1/8 inch thick. Cut out 2-inch shapes (stars, moons or small rounds) and place on an ungreased baking sheet. Repeat with remaining portions of dough.

BEAT egg with a pinch of salt in a small bowl. Brush egg glaze on cookies and sprinkle with nuts, coarsely cracked pepper or coriander, or fennel seeds.

BAKE for about 8 minutes, or until pale gold. Transfer cookies to a rack to cool. Serve at room temperature. Store in an airtight container.

Smoked Salmon Nori Rolls

MAKES ABOUT 24 PIECES

Hors d'oeuvres are little nibbles that whet your appetite before the main event. They should be simple and small enough not to spoil a guest's appetite, so delicious and spectacular-looking little munchies like these are perfect.

These are beautiful to look at and very tasty (they look like sushi but contain no rice). Serve them as an hors d'oeuvre or on a small salad of mixed greens as a first course.

1 cup thinly sliced red onions	$1/3$ cup whipping cream
$1/2$ tsp salt	1 tbsp wasabi paste
$1/2$ tsp granulated sugar	1 cup chopped arugula
1 tbsp red wine vinegar	10 oz (300 g) smoked salmon, thinly sliced
1 cup soft goat cheese	4 sheets nori

PLACE red onions in a bowl. Toss with salt, sugar and vinegar. Marinate for 2 hours at room temperature, or until onions are soft and slightly pickled.

BEAT together goat cheese, whipping cream and wasabi in a separate bowl until smooth. Stir in arugula.

PLACE a sheet of plastic wrap on counter. Lay about 4 pieces of smoked salmon on wrap, overlapping them to make a rectangle. Lay a sheet of nori on top and trim to fit salmon.

SPREAD goat cheese mixture over nori, leaving a $1/2$-inch border along one long edge of nori. Sprinkle pickled onions in a line about 1 inch from bottom edge. (This should put onions in centre of roll.)

LIFT edge of salmon and nori and roll tightly around onions toward the unfilled edge, using plastic wrap as a guide. Continue until you have a neat log. Repeat with remaining ingredients.

WRAP each log in plastic wrap and chill for at least 1 hour. Before serving, using a sharp knife, cut each log into $3/4$-inch pieces.

{ nori }

Nori is thin sheets of seaweed (or, more properly, marine algae) used in sushi. Keep it stored in the cupboard in an airtight container (I use a plastic zipper bag).

Dill and Scallion Pancakes

MAKES ABOUT 40 MINI PANCAKES

These baby pancakes make terrific bases for all kinds of hors d'oeuvres. Try topping them with a little sour cream, chopped red onion and prosciutto, smoked salmon or caviar. They can be served cold or reheated in a 300 F oven for 5 minutes.

½ cup all-purpose flour	1 tbsp butter, melted
1 tsp baking powder	¼ cup chopped green onions
½ tsp salt	2 tbsp chopped fresh dill
1 egg	2 tbsp vegetable oil
½ cup milk	

COMBINE flour, baking powder and salt in a bowl.

BEAT egg, milk and melted butter in a separate bowl. Stir egg mixture into flour mixture until combined. Stir in green onions and dill.

HEAT oil in a large non-stick skillet or griddle over medium heat. Add batter to skillet, using about 1 tsp batter per pancake. Cook for 1 minute, or until mixture is bubbly on top. Turn and cook second side for another minute, or until golden. Remove pancakes to a rack to cool, unless you are using them right away. Repeat with remaining batter.

{ hors d'oeuvres }

One challenge with hors d'oeuvres is finding a base that does not overwhelm the topping and takes little time to prepare. I often use vegetables such as Belgian endive, Bibb or Boston lettuce leaves, small iceberg lettuce cups, hollowed-out cherry tomatoes or baby patty pan squash.

It can be difficult to find a good commercial bread or cracker to serve with hors d'oeuvres. I avoid Melba toast (too crunchy and boring), pumpernickel squares (too overwhelming in flavour) and rice crackers (tasteless and crumbly). But it is easy to make your own toasts to use as a base for spreads or smoked salmon.

BAGUETTE TOASTS • Slice a baguette into thin slices on the diagonal. Place slices on an oiled baking sheet and bake at 350 F for 5 minutes. Turn toasts and bake for 5 minutes longer; they should be golden on both sides.

Cooking well is much easier if you have good equipment. You don't need lots of things, but good knives and a few good pots and pans are important.

KNIVES • At the minimum you should have a good chef's knife (with either an 8- or 10-inch blade), a paring knife, a serrated-edged knife for cutting fruit, and a slicing knife that can double as a carving knife. Before you buy, hold the knife to make sure it feels comfortable in your hand.

With the Japanese mounting a strong challenge to European knives, the hot new knife is a santoku—a cross between a cleaver and a chef's knife. It is made in both Japan and Europe, is very easy to handle and has good weight. The wider, shorter blade works well for moving ingredients from the chopping block to the pan. It is excellent for chopping, cutting and slicing because of its heft (good for cutting up a chicken, for example). It's a good all-purpose choice, although I still prefer a chef's knife.

Keep your knives very sharp by touching them up with a knife-sharpening steel before using. (You cut yourself less on sharp knives than you do on dull ones.)

POTS AND PANS • I prefer heavy pots with a bonded coating. The coating does not necessarily make them non-stick, but food does not adhere as easily. I also love copper pots and pans, but they are impractical for the home cook. They are expensive, difficult to keep clean and must be used with caution as they absorb and retain heat so well.

For a basic kitchen you need a large pot for stocks and pasta, a medium pot for vegetables and a smaller pot for sauces.

I use both regular and non-stick skillets. Non-stick are good for cooking eggs, pancakes and other foods that tend to stick, but they are not good for making sauces, because you need the little bits that stick to the bottom of a skillet after sautéing the main ingredients to add flavour to a sauce. They also do not work for caramel.

I also often use a sauté pan—a skillet with high, straight sides. It is useful for sautéing larger quantities, and for making stews.

Frequently I call for food to be seared on the stove and then baked in the oven. For these recipes, an ovenproof skillet works perfectly, and it cuts down on the cleanup. Just take care not to burn yourself when you take the pan out of the oven, and keep the handle covered until it cools down (I usually slip an oven mitt over the handle).

Smoked Trout, Avocado and Apple Salad

SERVES 4

A sexy salad with lots of different textures, based on an idea from my friend Simmy Clarke, with whom I have shared countless dinners.

8 oz (250 g) boneless smoked trout
1 green apple
2 tsp lemon juice
1 avocado
4 cups watercress leaves

Apple Cider Horseradish Dressing
2 tbsp cider vinegar
2 tsp mayonnaise
1 tsp prepared horseradish
1 tsp honey
$\frac{1}{4}$ cup olive oil
Salt and freshly ground pepper
2 tbsp chopped chives

FLAKE trout into large pieces.

CUT apple into matchsticks and toss with 1 tsp lemon juice.

SLICE avocado and toss separately with remaining 1 tsp lemon juice.

ARRANGE watercress on individual serving plates. Top with trout and apples. Garnish with avocado.

PREPARE dressing by whisking vinegar, mayonnaise, horseradish and honey in a bowl. Whisk in oil and season with salt and pepper.

DRIZZLE dressing over salad. Sprinkle salad with chopped chives.

{ avocadoes }

To ripen an avocado quickly, place it in a paper bag with a slice of apple and leave in a warm place.

To remove the flesh from the peel, cut the avocado in half lengthwise. Stick a knife blade into the pit and ease out the pit.

Using a large, oval-shaped spoon, scoop out the flesh of each half in one piece.

Avocado flesh oxidizes and turns dark when it is exposed to the air, so brush it with a few drops of lemon juice after scooping it out of the skin.

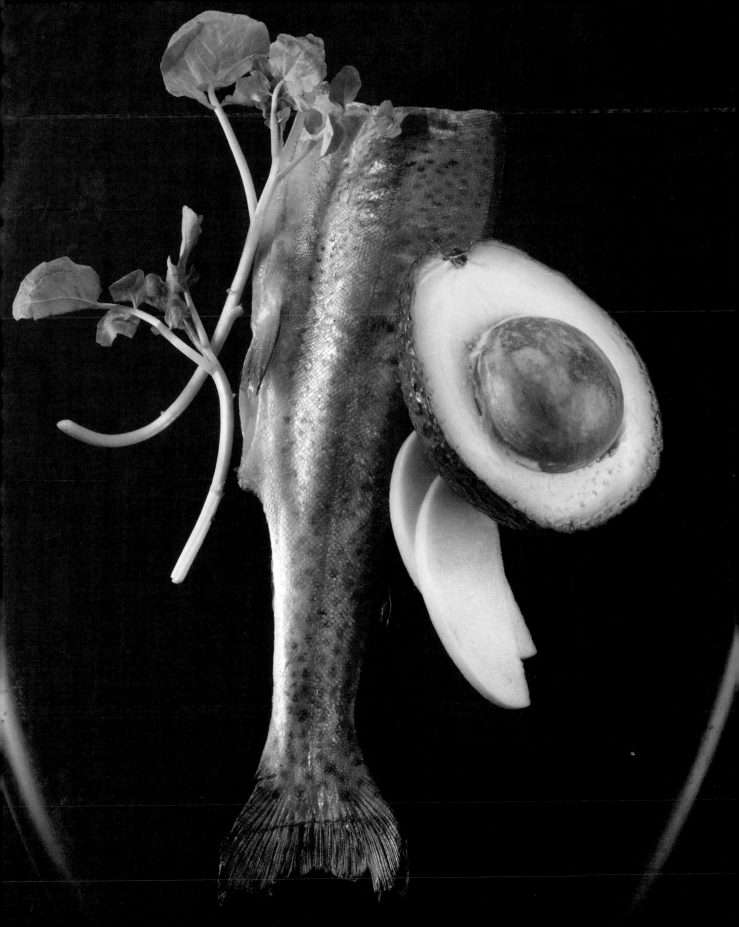

Squid Caesar Salad

SERVES 4

I love the crunch, crackle and crispness of deep-fried food. It is very addictive. This first course is a knockout, combining two favourites—fried squid (calamari) and Caesar salad. You can substitute shrimp for the calamari, but sauté them instead of deep-frying. Buy cleaned squid to save yourself a lot of trouble.

½ cup diced pancetta or bacon
1 small head Romaine lettuce, torn
Freshly ground pepper

Caesar Dressing
¼ cup mayonnaise
2 tbsp sour cream
3 tbsp lemon juice
1 tsp minced garlic
1 tsp Worcestershire sauce
3 anchovy fillets, chopped
½ cup olive oil
½ cup grated Parmesan cheese

Squid
1 egg
1 cup soda water
1 cup all-purpose flour
¾ tsp salt
Freshly ground pepper
12 oz (375 g) squid tubes
Vegetable oil for deep-frying

PLACE pancetta in a small, cold skillet. Heat skillet over medium heat and cook pancetta for 4 to 5 minutes, or until crisp. Drain on paper towels.

PLACE lettuce in a bowl and toss with pancetta. Season with pepper.

PREPARE dressing by combining mayonnaise, sour cream, lemon juice, garlic, Worcestershire sauce and anchovies in a separate bowl. Slowly whisk in olive oil. Stir in ¼ cup Parmesan cheese.

PREPARE batter for squid by whisking egg and soda water in a bowl. Slowly whisk in flour. Season with salt and pepper (just ignore any lumps).

DRY squid with a paper towels and cut tubes into ¼-inch slices. Drop into batter.

POUR oil into a wok or skillet until ½ inch deep and heat over medium-high heat. When a cube of bread turns brown in 15 seconds, oil is ready. Add squid in batches and fry for about 1 to 2 minutes, or until golden. Drain on paper towels.

TOSS lettuce and pancetta with dressing. Top with squid and remaining ¼ cup Parmesan.

{ deep-frying }

Don't be afraid of deep-frying. If food is deep-fried at the proper temperature, a minuscule amount of oil is absorbed, leaving the food crisp on the outside and steamed in its own juices inside.

Use a deep, heavy pan. (A wok sitting on a wok ring is excellent because its conical shape will prevent hot oil from spilling over, but any deep skillet or pot that has a narrower base than rim will work.) Chopsticks or long-handled metal tongs are necessary for turning food; you can also use two spatulas to turn larger pieces.

Use canola or peanut oil for deep-frying. They have a higher flash point than other oils, and are less likely to catch fire. The oil should be heated to 350 F. If the oil temperature is too low, the food will absorb the oil. The best way to test the temperature is to use a frying thermometer. A less reliable method is to drop a bread cube into the oil; if it browns in 15 seconds, the oil is ready.

Add room temperature food to the oil (refrigerated food will lower the oil temperature too much) and don't add too much food at once (this will also lower the temperature, and the food will become soggy). If you're worried about splattering, use a splatter screen.

Drain large pieces on a rack placed over a baking sheet. Use paper towels to drain smaller pieces, such as French fries, or to drain food that has absorbed a lot of oil.

To reheat deep-fried foods and keep them crisp, place them on a rack over a baking sheet to allow air circulation and reheat in a 400 F oven for 5 to 10 minutes, or until hot.

Spanish Cheese Fritters

MAKES ABOUT 20 FRITTERS

These are a total indulgence—the kind of food that you just can't stop eating.

The fritters can be reheated in a 350 F oven for 5 minutes, but they taste best right out of the pan.

Serve these on their own or, even better, with a spicy tomato sauce.

3 eggs
¼ cup milk
¼ cup all-purpose flour
1 tsp smoked paprika, or a pinch cayenne
1 ½ cups grated Manchego or Cheddar cheese

2 tbsp chopped parsley
¾ tsp salt
Freshly ground pepper
Vegetable oil for frying

WHISK eggs, milk, flour and paprika in a bowl. Stir in cheese, parsley, salt and pepper.

HEAT a large, deep skillet over medium heat. Add oil until ½ inch deep and heat. Use a tablespoon to drop batter into oil in batches. Cook for 30 seconds per side, or until fritters are golden brown.

DRAIN fritters on paper towels and serve warm.

{ spicy tomato sauce }

Heat 1 tbsp olive oil in a pot over medium heat. Add 4 anchovy fillets and 1 tsp chopped garlic and sauté for 1 minute, or until anchovies begin to melt. Stir in 4 chopped tomatoes (or 1½ cups chopped canned tomatoes) and 1 tsp chili flakes. Bring to a boil, reduce heat to low, cover and cook for 10 minutes.

Puree sauce with a hand blender. Season with salt and pepper if necessary.

Makes about 1 cup.

{ paprika }

Paprika is a ground red pepper powder that varies in taste, depending on the pepper. Hungarian paprika is strong and earthy, while Spanish paprika ranges from mild to very hot. Very trendy right now is smoked Spanish paprika, which adds an intense smoky flavour to dishes.

Paprika only becomes flavourful when it is heated, so sprinkling it on food after cooking will not add any taste.

Mushroom Rolls

MAKES ABOUT 20 PIECES

An easy hors d'oeuvre (or snack if there are any leftovers!). Serve the pieces standing upright on a tray.

You could use all brown mushrooms in this; chop them finely (a food processor works well). Please use an inexpensive white sandwich bread that can be rolled out very thinly.

3 tbsp butter	2 tbsp finely chopped parsley
6 oz (175 g) brown mushrooms, chopped	Salt and freshly ground pepper
4 oz (125 g) shiitake mushrooms, chopped	6 slices white sandwich bread
1 tsp finely chopped garlic	2 tbsp olive oil
1/3 cup whipping cream	1/3 cup grated Cheddar cheese
1 tbsp soy sauce	

PREHEAT oven to 400 F.

HEAT butter in a large skillet over high heat. Add brown and shiitake mushrooms and sauté for about 2 minutes, or until juices appear.

ADD garlic and sauté for 2 minutes longer, or until juices disappear. Add cream and soy sauce and continue to cook for about 1 minute, or until cream just coats mushrooms. Add parsley and season well with salt and pepper. Let cool.

CUT crusts off bread. With a rolling pin, roll out each bread slice thinly. Brush one side of bread with oil. Turn slices oiled side down.

SPREAD about 2 tbsp mushroom filling over each bread slice, leaving a 1/2-inch border along side farthest from you. Sprinkle mushrooms with grated cheese.

ROLL up bread away from you to enclose filling. Place seam side down on a baking sheet and bake for 5 minutes. Turn rolls and bake for 5 minutes longer, or until bread is golden and cheese melts. Let cool slightly before cutting on diagonal into slices 1 inch thick.

Cornmeal-fried Oysters with Chipotle Mayonnaise

SERVES 4

Everyone loves fried oysters, and this Cajun dish is perfect at Christmas, or at any other time of the year. Buy shucked oysters to save time and trouble. If you buy the larger BC oysters for this dish, cut them in half.

Serve the oysters on a bed of watercress as a first course.

Chipotle Mayonnaise	Oysters
1/2 cup mayonnaise	1/2 cup cornmeal
1 tsp chopped chipotles	1/2 cup all-purpose flour
1 tsp adobo sauce	1 tsp paprika
Salt	1 tsp dried thyme
2 tbsp chopped fresh coriander	Salt and freshly ground pepper
	16 shucked oysters
	1/4 cup vegetable oil, approx.

COMBINE mayonnaise, chipotles and adobo sauce in a bowl. Season with salt and stir in coriander.

COMBINE cornmeal, flour, paprika, thyme, salt and pepper in a dish. Toss oysters in cornmeal mixture.

HEAT a large skillet over high heat. Add enough oil to film base of skillet. When oil is very hot, add oysters, but do not crowd pan. Fry on one side for 30 seconds, or until browned. Turn oysters and fry second side. Remove immediately to a serving dish. Add more oil as needed to fry remaining oysters. Serve with chipotle mayonnaise.

{ chipotles }

Chipotles in adobo
sauce are smoked jalapeños preserved in a very spicy tomato sauce. Both the peppers and the sauce are used in some dishes. Chipotles are sold in cans and are available in Mexican or South American stores and in upscale grocery stores. If you can't find them, you can substitute hot Asian chili sauce, though you will lose the smoky flavour.

Mini Crabcakes with Garlic Mayonnaise

MAKES ABOUT 36 CRABCAKES

This is one of the most-requested recipes I have ever created. The crabcakes are baked, not fried. Serve them on a lettuce leaf with a dab of garlic mayonnaise as an hors d'oeuvre, or as a first course.

$^1/_4$ cup mayonnaise

1 egg yolk

1 tbsp Dijon mustard

2 tsp lemon juice

$^1/_2$ tsp Worcestershire sauce

$^1/_4$ cup chopped green onions

$^1/_4$ cup chopped roasted red peppers

2 tbsp chopped fresh coriander

1 lb (500 g) crabmeat, defrosted if frozen and
    squeezed dry

Salt and freshly ground pepper

$^1/_2$ tsp hot pepper sauce

$^1/_2$ cup cornmeal

$^1/_2$ cup all-purpose flour

3 tbsp butter, melted

Garlic Mayonnaise

$^1/_2$ cup mayonnaise

1 tbsp lemon juice

1 tsp minced garlic

$^1/_2$ tsp hot pepper sauce

2 tbsp chopped fresh coriander

Salt and freshly ground pepper

PREHEAT oven to 450 F.

COMBINE mayonnaise, egg yolk, mustard, lemon juice, Worcestershire, green onions, red peppers and coriander in a bowl. Flake crabmeat and stir in. Season with salt, pepper and hot pepper sauce. Form mixture into 1-inch balls and flatten slightly.

COMBINE cornmeal and flour on a plate. Roll crab balls in cornmeal/flour mixture.

BRUSH a baking sheet with melted butter. Arrange crabcakes on baking sheet and drizzle with remaining butter.

BAKE crabcakes for 7 minutes. Turn and cook for 7 to 8 minutes longer, or until crisp.

PREPARE mayonnaise while crabcakes are baking. Whisk mayonnaise, lemon juice, garlic, hot pepper sauce and coriander in a bowl. Thin with water if too thick. Season with salt and pepper. Serve garlic mayonnaise with crabcakes.

Seared Scallop Ceviche

SERVES 4

Ceviche is usually fresh raw fish that is "cooked" in lime juice. My version sears the scallops first to add texture and flavour to the dish. Don't leave the scallops in the marinade for more than four hours, though, or they will overcook!

2 tbsp olive oil	³⁄₄ cup chopped red peppers
1 lb (500 g) sea scallops	³⁄₄ cup chopped red onions
Salt and freshly ground pepper	2 tsp finely chopped jalapeño
¹⁄₄ cup orange juice	3 tbsp chopped fresh coriander
¹⁄₂ cup lime juice	

HEAT oil in a large non-stick skillet over high heat. Add scallops and sauté for 1 minute per side, or until seared. Season with salt and pepper and cut into quarters.

COMBINE orange juice, lime juice, red peppers, onions, jalapeño, coriander and scallops in a bowl. Marinate for 1 to 4 hours, refrigerated, before serving.

SERVE the scallops sprinkled with a little marinade on Boston lettuce.

{ scallops }

Scallops actually grow in the beautiful fan-shaped shells that are often used for serving. In Europe scallops are sold in the shell with the roe attached; the roe is a real delicacy, and it's a shame our scallops are not sold the same way. However, even shelled scallops usually include the muscle that attaches the scallop to the shell, and this muscle should be removed before cooking, as it is tough. You can easily pull it off with your fingers. Scallops, like shrimp, come in many different sizes. Bay scallops are tiny and often tasteless. Other scallops are graded by size (the largest come about 6–10 to a pound).

Scallops should be shiny, bright and dry when you buy them.

Grilled Shrimp with Double Horseradish Dip

SERVES 6

This is much more interesting than shrimp with a ketchup-like cocktail sauce. The horse-radish dip is spicy but not overwhelming (you can also serve it with fried chicken and vegetables). Pile the shrimp on a plate and place the dip in the centre.

You can cook the shrimp on the barbecue or in a grill pan.

1/4 cup olive oil	**Double Horseradish Dip**
2 tbsp red wine vinegar	1/4 cup sour cream or mayonnaise
2 tbsp soy sauce	2 tbsp plain yogurt
2 tsp wasabi paste	2 tbsp prepared horseradish
1 tsp granulated sugar	1 tbsp wasabi paste
1 tsp finely chopped gingerroot	1 tbsp chopped chives
1 tsp grated lemon rind	Salt to taste
1 1/2 lb (750 g) large shrimp, peeled	
Salt to taste	

COMBINE oil, vinegar, soy sauce, wasabi, sugar, ginger and lemon rind in a large bowl. Add shrimp and toss to coat. Marinate for 30 minutes at room temperature.

PREPARE dip while shrimp are marinating. In a bowl, whisk together sour cream, yogurt, horseradish and wasabi. Stir in chives. Season with salt.

REMOVE shrimp from marinade. Season with salt and thread onto skewers, making sure skewers go through shrimp body twice so shrimp are easy to turn and do not flop around.

PREHEAT grill on high. Grill shrimp for 1 to 2 minutes per side, or until pink and just cooked through. Remove from skewers and serve with dip.

{ wasabi }

Bright-green wasabi is also known as Japanese horseradish, although it is

not really a horseradish. It is very hot and usually served with sushi. The knobby green root grows in Japan but is hardly ever available fresh. Buy it in powdered form and mix with an equal amount of water, or buy the less intensely flavoured paste that comes premixed in a tube.

Spanish Tortilla

SERVES 8

When I was in Spain many years ago, I fell in love with tapas—lots of little plates containing great-tasting nibbles to eat with drinks. This has become a hot trend, and restaurants of all kinds are now serving small plates of food to pique the interest of diners.

This classic Spanish tapas makes a good brunch dish as well as a first course or hors d'oeuvre.

¼ cup olive oil	Salt and freshly ground pepper
½ cup chopped onions	1 tsp smoked paprika
1 tsp chopped garlic	6 eggs
1 lb (500 g) Yukon Gold potatoes, peeled and cut in ½-inch dice	1 tbsp chopped parsley

HEAT oil in a 9-inch non-stick ovenproof skillet over medium heat. Add onions, garlic and potatoes and season with salt and pepper. Sauté for 10 minutes, or until potatoes are tender. Add paprika, tossing to coat. Spread potatoes evenly over bottom of pan.

PREHEAT broiler.

BEAT eggs with salt, pepper and parsley. Pour egg mixture over potatoes and spread evenly. Reduce heat to medium-low and cook until eggs are set on bottom and sides, about 5 minutes.

PLACE skillet under broiler for 2 minutes, or until eggs are nicely browned and cooked through.

INVERT tortilla onto a plate and cool to room temperature. Cut into 8 wedges.

Oeufs en Cocotte

SERVES 4

When I was last in Paris, I ate at a casual but exquisite restaurant—L'atelier de Joël Robuchon—where you sat at the counter surrounding the kitchen and discussed with the servers which dishes to choose. This recipe is based on a dish I had there.

A fashionable appetizer in Europe, this is perfect for home entertaining. These are basically eggs baked in small gratin dishes. At Joël Robuchon's the eggs were served in heatproof martini glasses, but you can use any small ovenproof dishes (we used votive candle holders).

4 eggs
2 tbsp butter
6 oz (175 g) mixed mushrooms, sliced
4 cups baby spinach

1 cup whipping cream
Salt and freshly ground pepper
2 drops truffle oil

PREHEAT oven to 300 F.

BREAK eggs into four buttered 1-cup ramekins. Place a tiny knob of butter on each egg.

PLACE ramekins in a deep baking dish large enough to hold all ramekins. Fill baking dish with boiling water until it comes halfway up sides of ramekins. Place baking dish in oven and bake eggs for 8 to 10 minutes, or until egg yolks are just set but still runny. (Eggs will continue to cook after sauce has been added.)

PREPARE sauce while eggs are cooking. Heat remaining butter in a large skillet over high heat. Add mushrooms and sauté for about 3 minutes, or until just cooked. Add spinach and cook for 1 minute, or just until spinach wilts.

ADD cream to skillet and bring to a boil. Season with salt and pepper and add a drop or two of truffle oil.

SPOON mushroom mixture over eggs. Remove from water bath and serve at once.

{ water bath }

Food is cooked in a water bath (*bain marie*) when you want to poach delicate ingredients in the oven or on top of the stove so that they set but do not overcook. The gentle heat means cheesecakes are less likely to crack, and custards don't get crusty.

Place the baking dish or dishes in a roasting pan. Before cooking, pour boiling water into the roasting pan until the water comes halfway up the sides of the baking dish.

Imperial Mushroom Compote

SERVES 4

For an elegant first course, spoon the mushrooms over a small salad of bitter greens such as frisee or arugula, or serve on toasts as an hors d'oeuvre.

The miso thickens the sauce naturally and gives the dish a sweet, earthy taste.

2 tbsp vegetable oil	¼ cup light miso
1 tsp sesame oil	¼ cup whipping cream
2 tbsp chopped shallots	1 tbsp soy sauce
1 tbsp chopped gingerroot	Salt and freshly ground pepper
1 tbsp chopped garlic	1 tbsp chopped parsley
1 lb (500 g) mixed mushrooms, sliced	1 tbsp chopped chives

HEAT vegetable oil and sesame oil in a large skillet or sauté pan over medium heat. Add shallots, ginger and garlic and stir-fry for 30 seconds.

ADD mushrooms and sauté for about 3 minutes, or until mushrooms are softened and juicy.

STIR in miso, cream and soy sauce and bring to a boil. Season with salt and pepper and scatter with parsley and chives.

{ miso }

Miso is Japanese fermented soybean paste. It has a unique taste—slightly salty and fragrant—and is high in protein, amino acids, vitamins and minerals and very low in calories and fat. The Japanese have always regarded miso as a health food and cancer fighter. Look for it in the refrigerated health food section of the supermarket.

The key to using miso is balance. Too much can overwhelm a dish.

Light or white miso is delicate in texture and probably best suits North American palates. Try it in salad dressings instead of oil (page 59) or as a flavour energizer in soups, sauces and vegetable dishes.

Darker red or brown miso is best used in heartier dishes. It goes well with strong soups, beans and lentils.

Miso will keep, refrigerated, for one year, but once opened it does become darker and stronger over time.

Caramelized Onion and Goat Cheese Tarts

SERVES 4

Simple but spectacular. Use homemade or storebought pastry shells, or wonton nests. (Wonton nests are usually used with cold fillings, but in this case the mixture only warms for 5 minutes.) If you don't want to make the tomato chili jam, substitute a thick tomato or fig chutney.

Salting the onions when they go into the pan helps the caramelization by drawing out the onion juices.

$1/4$ cup olive oil	4 prebaked 4-inch tart shells
2 cups sliced onions	$1/2$ cup tomato chili jam (page 35)
Salt and freshly ground pepper	6 cups baby lettuce
$1/2$ cup soft goat cheese	1 tbsp lemon juice

HEAT 2 tbsp oil in a large skillet over medium-low heat. Add onions and salt and cook, stirring occasionally, for 20 minutes, or until onions are well browned and very soft. Season with pepper.

PREHEAT oven to 350 F.

SPREAD goat cheese in bottom of each tart shell. Top with caramelized onions and a spoonful of tomato chili jam.

PLACE tarts in oven for 5 minutes to warm.

TOSS baby lettuce with remaining oil and lemon juice and pile on top of tartlets.

{ wonton nests }

Make these easy tart shells to hold cold fillings such as hummos. Wonton wrappers are available at supermarkets and Asian grocery stores. The thicker wrappers make the best nests (some wrappers are so thin and transparent that you can see through them).

Separate wonton wrappers and brush one side with melted butter. Fit the wrappers, buttered side down, into the cups of a mini muffin pan, letting the sides of the wrappers fold and ruffle slightly. Bake in a preheated 350 F oven for 7 minutes, or until pale gold.

{ tomato chili jam }

This excellent "jam" also makes a great condiment for curries, cold meats, sandwiches and cream cheese on a bagel. It keeps for a month, refrigerated.

Drain a 28-oz (796 mL) can tomatoes. Puree half the tomatoes in a food processor with 2 tbsp chopped gingerroot, 2 tsp chopped garlic, 2 tbsp fish sauce and ½ tsp hot Asian chili sauce. Chop remaining tomatoes.

Combine tomato puree in a deep pot with 1 cup brown sugar and ¾ cup red wine vinegar. Slowly bring to a boil, stirring constantly. Add chopped tomatoes, reduce heat and simmer gently for 30 to 40 minutes, or until mixture is dark red and jam-like. Cool and refrigerate.

Makes 2 cups.

{ onions }

COOKING ONIONS • Also called yellow onions, these are strong-tasting, and they are the onions most likely to make you cry when you chop them. I prefer to use Spanish onions because they are larger (less peeling and more onion) and slightly milder.

VIDALIA ONIONS • Very sweet onions from the southern United States. They caramelize well and are great in sandwiches and salads, but I find them a bit mild for regular cooking.

RED ONIONS • Milder than cooking onions, they are sweet and add beautiful colour to salads and garnishes. When cooked they have a pink hue; they are especially fine when grilled.

SHALLOTS • Elongated or round, sometimes with two or three clove clusters. They are not as strongly flavoured as regular onions and in fact impart a slight sweetness to dishes. They are good in salad dressings and sauces.

GREEN ONIONS • Also known as spring onions or scallions, they are mild, with white bulbs and green stalks. Use them in salads and as a garnish.

Spinach and Leek Strata

SERVES 8 TO 10

Stratas are like crustless quiches, with bread added to give them body. They are always a big hit as long as they contain enough egg and cream to give the bread a really good soak. They are easy to make, and I always put them together a day ahead.

Use the least expensive white or egg sandwich bread, otherwise the strata will be too bready. I serve it with a salad as a first course, but it is also my brunch dish for all occasions. Change the cheeses, substitute mushrooms for the leeks, or add diced cooked bacon, sausages or prosciutto—it is a freehand dish.

2 tbsp olive oil	1 cup grated Parmesan cheese
1 bunch leeks, trimmed and chopped	6 eggs
2 bunches spinach, stemmed and sliced	3 cups cream or milk
Salt and freshly ground pepper	2 tbsp Dijon mustard
10 to 12 slices bread, crusts removed	$\frac{1}{2}$ tsp hot pepper sauce, or to taste
2 tbsp butter, softened	$\frac{1}{2}$ cup chopped chives
3 cups grated Cheddar cheese	2 tsp paprika

HEAT oil in a large skillet over medium-high heat. Add leeks and sauté for 3 minutes, or until softened. Add spinach, stir together and cook for 2 minutes, or until spinach wilts. Season with salt and pepper.

ARRANGE a layer of bread over bottom of a large buttered baking dish. Brush with butter. Spread half the vegetable mixture over bread. Sprinkle half the Cheddar and half the Parmesan over vegetables. Add a second layer of bread and brush with remaining butter. Add remaining vegetables and cover with remaining cheese.

WHISK eggs, cream, mustard, hot pepper sauce and chives in a bowl. Season well with salt and pepper.

POUR egg mixture over vegetables. Let sit for 1 hour or refrigerate, covered, overnight.

PREHEAT oven to 350 F. Let strata come to room temperature.

SPRINKLE strata with paprika and bake for 45 minutes, or until puffed. Cool for 10 minutes before serving.

{ soups }

Chicken Stock

MAKES ABOUT 12 CUPS

My mother always had a stock pot bubbling on the stove. Every day she would throw in a few odds and ends, some water or wine and bring it all back to the boil. We were a bit scared of this pot because we had no idea how long it had been around, although Mother assured us that she did wash the pot every time we moved!

When I make stock, I often poach a small chicken in the water for about an hour, remove the meat for eating and then return the bones to the pot for an even richer stock.

4 lb (2 kg) chicken bones	3 stalks celery, cut in chunks
16 cups cold water	3 unpeeled garlic cloves
2 unpeeled onions, quartered	6 whole peppercorns
3 large carrots, cut in chunks	

PLACE chicken bones in a large stock pot and cover with cold water. (Water should cover bones by 2 inches.) Bring to a boil. With a slotted spoon, skim off any foam and discard.

ADD onions, carrots, celery, garlic and peppercorns. Reduce heat and simmer gently, uncovered, for 4 hours, or until stock has reduced by one-third.

COOL stock and strain into a large bowl (discard vegetables). Cover and freeze or refrigerate (it will be easier to remove fat after chilling). Remove fat before using.

{ making stock }

Good soups start with good stock but, unfortunately, bouillon cubes have replaced stock pots in most modern kitchens.

Stocks are basic to good cooking. They are simple to prepare and add body and soul to soups and stews. Homemade stock also makes far better sauces, because it thickens naturally when it is reduced.

Chicken stock is the most versatile stock, as it can be used to replace beef or fish stock. It is the only one I make.

Use chicken backs and necks (they are the least expensive bones to buy), and add a few wings for extra flavour. Freeze any uncooked necks or bones from chickens you buy for other dishes for up to 6 months and toss them into your stock. Stock made with leftover cooked chicken, such as a roasted chicken carcass, will be a darker colour because the bones are cooked, but it will be full of flavour.

The best vegetables to include in stock are onions, carrots and celery (adding the onion

skins will give the stock a rich yellow colour). But don't worry about exact amounts—using more or less will not drastically affect the final result. You can also add parsnips for a sweeter flavour. Instead of discarding leek and green onion tops, freeze them and add them to stock. Mushroom stalks will also enrich the flavour.

Use whole peppercorns; ground pepper will cloud the liquid. And never salt stock during the cooking, because it can become too salty when reduced.

All stock should be started in cold water. Otherwise the albumin in the bones clouds the soup instead of rising to the top as as a grey scum that can be skimmed off when the stock comes to a boil.

Refrigerate strained stock for up to 5 days. The fat will congeal on top and help preserve it. To freeze stock, remove the congealed fat and freeze 1-cup or 2-cup portions in plastic bags.

Spicy Chicken Soup with Mushrooms and Lemon

SERVES 4

An easy Asian-themed soup that is good served before a heavier main course; I also make it as a quick pick-me-up for lunch.

5 cups chicken stock

6 shiitake mushrooms, stemmed and sliced

2 cups baby spinach

4 green onions, slivered

1 tbsp soy sauce

1 tbsp lemon juice

½ tsp hot Asian chili sauce

COMBINE stock and mushrooms in a pot and bring to a boil.

STIR in spinach, green onions, soy sauce, lemon juice and chili sauce. Simmer for 1 minute, or until spinach has wilted. Taste and adjust seasonings if necessary.

{ troubleshooting: soups }

Soup making is an easy and useful skill to learn, because anything edible can be turned into a soup. Simmer a handful of carrots in chicken stock with some curry powder; give second life to a few elderly zucchini by adding apples and watercress; combine leftover salad with canned kidney beans and pasta. The combinations are endless and exciting, so feel free to experiment.

If, however, your finished soup tastes uninteresting or underseasoned despite your creative efforts, there are a number of ways to rescue it:

- A dash or two of salt always improves a lacklustre flavour, and freshly ground pepper adds spice. (White pepper will keep white soups white, but if you don't have it, don't worry.) Cayenne adds heat and is especially effective in thick bean soups.
- A finely chopped small garlic clove added 10 minutes before the end of the cooking will prevent a soup from being flat.
- A spoonful of tomato paste will add body and flavour to any soup.
- A few pinches of curry powder will add a background flavour—not necessarily hot, but with more depth. Try adding it to a bland cream soup or bean soup.
- A few drops of fresh lemon or lime juice will liven up all soups.
- A teaspoon of chopped fresh tarragon, basil, chives or thyme will perk up a cream soup or tomato soup.

Mushroom and Barley Soup

SERVES 4

A rich soup for the cold weather. Serve it with a salad or sandwich or as a meal on its own.

1 tbsp olive oil

1/2 cup chopped onions

1/2 cup chopped carrots

1/2 cup chopped leeks

1 tsp chopped garlic

1/2 cup pearl barley

6 cups chicken stock

1/2 tsp dried marjoram

4 oz (125 g) brown mushrooms, sliced

3 cups baby spinach

Salt and freshly ground pepper

HEAT oil in a pot over medium heat. Add onions, carrots, leeks and garlic. Sauté for 1 minute, then add barley and stir to coat with oil.

ADD stock and marjoram, bring to a boil, reduce heat and simmer for 30 minutes, or until barley is almost tender.

STIR in mushrooms and spinach and cook for 10 minutes, or until barley is tender. Season well with salt and pepper.

{ stock substitutes }

Today there are many good stock substitutes available, ranging from the stock your butcher makes to vegetarian and organic stocks sold in Tetra Paks at the supermarket. Look for a low-salt version if you are going to reduce the stock in sauces.

The concentrated refrigerated stock sold as a paste is also very good. Look for products that have chicken as the first ingredient and do not contain MSG.

If you can only find powdered or cubed instant stock, you can improve it in the following way. In a large pot, combine the instant stock with twice the amount of water called for. Add a sliced onion, carrot and stalk of celery. Bring to a boil, then simmer for 30 minutes. Strain before using.

Tomato Soup with Chickpeas and Swiss Chard

SERVES 6 TO 8

You can substitute kale for the chard, but add the kale to the pot at the same time as the garlic so it will cook a bit longer.

1 bunch Swiss chard	4 cups chicken stock
2 tbsp olive oil	1 tsp chopped fresh rosemary, or $1/4$ tsp dried
1 tbsp chopped garlic	$1/2$ tsp hot Asian chili sauce
1 cup chopped onions	1 19-oz (540 mL) can chickpeas, rinsed and drained
1 28-oz (796 mL) can tomatoes, chopped with juices	Salt and freshly ground pepper
	$1/2$ cup grated Parmesan cheese

CUT away stems and any tough or wide centre ribs from chard and slice them. Roughly chop leaves.

HEAT oil in a large pot over medium heat. Add garlic and sauté for 2 minutes, or until golden. Add onions and chard stems and ribs and sauté for 2 minutes, or until soft.

ADD tomatoes, stock, rosemary and chili sauce and simmer for 20 minutes. Add chickpeas and simmer for 15 minutes longer.

ADD chard leaves and simmer for 5 minutes, or until leaves wilt. Season well with salt and pepper. Serve sprinkled with Parmesan.

{ parmigiano reggiano }

Parmigiano Reggiano is the finest Parmesan cheese. It is produced in Emilia Romagna, Italy, under stringent conditions; in fact, real Parmesan will have its name and the date it was made stamped on the rind. Its depth of flavour and nutty, fragrant taste make it a wonderful cheese to eat and cook with. It melts beautifully and binds together other ingredients. Grate it as you need it, because it dries out once grated.

Grana Padano is another excellent Italian cheese for grating and cooking. It is made in a similar style to Reggiano, but is sweeter and less expensive. In Italy it is the most popular cheese served with pasta.

Don't buy the Parmesan cheese in a can. It has no taste. Keep fresh Parmesan wrapped in cheesecloth or waxed paper; plastic wrap will make it dry out. Use this method to keep all cheese fresh.

French Lentil Soup

SERVES 4

Use the small green French lentils—called lentils du Puy—if they are available. Otherwise use the larger brown lentils.

I like this healthy soup left a little chunky, but you can puree it completely if you wish.

1 head garlic, separated into cloves	1/4 cup chopped parsley
4 cups water	1 tbsp lemon juice
1/4 cup olive oil	Salt and freshly ground pepper
1 cup chopped onions	2 tbsp plain yogurt
1 cup lentils du Puy	1 tsp chili oil

COMBINE garlic and water in a pot and bring to a boil. Boil for 2 minutes. Drain, reserving cooking water. Peel garlic cloves.

HEAT 1 tbsp olive oil in a pot over medium heat. Add onions and garlic cloves and sauté for 3 minutes.

ADD lentils, reserved water and remaining 3 tbsp oil and bring to a boil. Cover and simmer for 30 to 45 minutes, or until lentils are soft.

PUREE soup (soup doesn't have to be completely smooth) and return to pot. Stir in parsley, lemon juice, salt and pepper and reheat. If soup is too thick, add a little water.

COMBINE yogurt and chili oil in a bowl and streak over soup when serving.

{ peeling garlic }

To peel large quantities of garlic easily, cut off the root end of the garlic head, separate the cloves and place in a small pot. Cover with water and bring to a boil. Drain. The skins will slip off.

Onion Bisque with Chili Oil

SERVES 6 TO 8

The combination of sweet onions and hot spice makes a superb soup. The soy sauce adds colour and a rich flavour. As an alternative to the chili oil, you could top the soup with grated cheese.

2 tbsp olive oil
3 cups thinly sliced red onions
2 cups thinly sliced Spanish onions
1 cup thinly sliced leeks
Pinch granulated sugar
Salt
1 tsp chopped garlic
1 tbsp balsamic vinegar

5 cups chicken stock
2 tbsp soy sauce
1½ tsp chopped fresh thyme,
     or ½ tsp dried
Freshly ground pepper
¼ cup whipping cream
2 tbsp chili oil

HEAT oil in a large pot over medium heat. Add onions, leeks, sugar and salt. Sauté gently for 5 minutes, or until onions are slightly softened.

ADD garlic and vinegar and continue to cook, stirring occasionally, until onions are very soft, about 20 minutes.

ADD stock, soy sauce, thyme and pepper and bring to a boil. Reduce heat and simmer for 10 minutes.

PUREE soup, return to pot and add cream. Simmer for 5 minutes to amalgamate flavours. Taste and adjust seasonings if necessary. Ladle soup into bowls and drizzle with chili oil.

{ chili oil }

You can buy chili oil in the supermarket, but it is easy to make your own. Add a little to spice up your cooking oil when you are sautéing, or drizzle it on pizza or grilled chicken. (This is a strong oil, so use it sparingly at first.)

In a small pot, combine 2 tbsp chili flakes and 1 cup olive oil. Bring to a simmer. Transfer oil and chili flakes to a glass jar, seal and let sit at room temperature for three days. Strain oil if you wish. It keeps unrefrigerated for one month.

Makes about 1 cup.

Spinach Borscht

SERVES 6

Traditionally spinach borscht is made with a mixture of spinach and sorrel—a lemony herb. Sorrel gives the soup a bright, zesty taste, but it is not always available, so if you can't find it, substitute 2 cups extra spinach and add an extra tablespoon of lemon juice.

2 tbsp butter	4 cups shredded spinach
1 cup chopped onions	2 cups shredded sorrel
1/4 cup chopped green onions	1/4 cup sour cream
1 cup diced Yukon Gold potatoes	1 tbsp lemon juice
5 cups chicken stock	Salt and freshly ground pepper

HEAT butter in a pot over medium-high heat. Add onions, green onions and potatoes and sauté for 3 minutes, or until onions soften.

STIR in stock and bring to a boil. Reduce heat and simmer, covered, for 10 minutes, or until potatoes are softened.

ADD spinach and sorrel and cook for another 5 minutes, or until spinach has wilted.

PUREE soup and return to pot. Add sour cream, lemon juice, salt and pepper and simmer for 2 to 3 minutes, or until flavours amalgamate. (Do not boil or the cream will curdle.)

{ thickening soups }

Green vegetables are lacking in starch, so a thickener is often added when they are used in cream soups. I find that flour and cornstarch detract from the natural flavours and produce a texture like canned soup, so I prefer to thicken soups with a root vegetable such as potatoes, which add body and smoothness without detracting from the flavour or texture. Use Yukon Gold or baking potatoes. Other starchy vegetables such as turnips, sweet potatoes and Jerusalem artichokes work well, too.

Another thickening technique is to increase the proportion of vegetables to liquid. The soup will have a more intense flavour and lighter consistency than one thickened with potatoes.

Adding cream mellows the flavour of a soup and adds richness, but you can always omit it if you like the flavour without it, or to reduce calories. I usually use a small amount of whipping cream, because it is the only cream that does not curdle when boiled. If you use yogurt, buttermilk or sour cream, do not bring the soup to a boil, or it will curdle.

Fennel and Orange Soup

SERVES 6

The combination of fennel and orange gives this soup loads of character. It is also very easy to make.

I like to roast vegetables for soups because roasting gives the soup a more intense and complex taste, but if time is short, you can omit this step.

2 bulbs fennel, trimmed	$\frac{1}{2}$ cup orange juice
2 tbsp olive oil	$\frac{1}{4}$ cup whipping cream
1 cup chopped onions	Salt and freshly ground pepper
1 tsp ground fennel seeds	2 tbsp sliced almonds, toasted
3 cups chicken stock	

PREHEAT oven to 400 F.

CUT each fennel bulb into quarters and brush with about 1 tbsp oil. Place on a baking sheet and roast for 20 minutes, or until golden and tender.

HEAT remaining 1 tbsp oil in a large pot over medium heat. Add onions and ground fennel seeds and sauté for 4 minutes, or until onions are softened.

CHOP roasted fennel and add to onions with stock and orange juice. Bring to a boil, cover and simmer for 15 minutes, or until fennel is very soft.

PUREE soup and return to pot. Add cream, bring to a boil and simmer for 5 minutes, adding stock if soup is too thick. Season with salt and pepper. Serve garnished with almonds.

{ fennel }

Fennel is a bulbous vegetable that has a slight licorice flavour. Trim the stem end and cut off any stalks from the top of the bulb. Remove the tough little core before slicing. The feathery fronds have a passing acquaintance to dill and can be used as a flavouring or garnish.

Watercress Soup

SERVES 4
A fabulous peppery soup to serve before a rich meal.

2 tbsp butter

$\frac{1}{2}$ cup diced Yukon Gold potatoes

$\frac{1}{2}$ cup chopped onions

Salt and freshly ground pepper

$1\frac{1}{4}$ cups chicken stock or water

$1\frac{1}{4}$ cups milk

2 bunches watercress, trimmed and chopped

HEAT butter in a pot over medium-low heat. Add potatoes and onions and toss until coated. Sprinkle with salt and pepper.

COVER and cook for 10 minutes. Add stock and milk and cook gently until potatoes are soft, about 5 to 8 minutes.

ADD watercress and simmer for 3 to 4 minutes, or until watercress is cooked. Do not over-cook or soup will lose its fresh green colour.

PUREE soup and return to pot. Reheat and adjust seasonings, but do not boil before serving.

{ watercress }

Watercress is a member of the nasturtium family, and it grows on the banks of streams. It has a distinctive spicy flavour and is good in salads and sandwiches.

Store it upside-down with its leaves in a bowl of water. It should stay fresh for more than a week.

Mushroom Cappuccino

SERVES 4

Trendy restaurants are serving soups that are foamed, and you can achieve a similar texture at home by using a milk frother or hand blender.

2 tbsp butter	4 cups chicken stock
1 cup chopped onions	$\frac{1}{2}$ cup whipping cream
1 cup chopped leeks (white part only)	Salt and freshly ground pepper
1 lb (500 g) mixed mushrooms, chopped	

HEAT butter in a pot over medium heat. Add onions, leeks and mushrooms and sauté for about 3 minutes, or until vegetables are softened.

ADD stock and bring to a boil. Simmer for 10 minutes, or until all vegetables are cooked.

PUREE soup and return to pot. Add cream and reheat. Season with salt and pepper.

FROTH soup using a frother or hand blender and pour into soup bowls or coffee cups.

{ blenders }

Hand blenders do not puree as well as countertop blenders, but I think they are great kitchen tools. They can be used to froth cream or to blend soups, sauces, dips and salad dressings. Look for a hand blender with a strong motor and sharp blades.

The food processor does not puree soups as well as a blender, but I often use it for convenience, because my blender is hidden in a cupboard, while the food processor sits on the counter!

Roasted Asparagus Soup

SERVES 4 TO 6

I only serve asparagus when it is in season, so this soup is a great early-summer treat. (We eat so much asparagus when it is available locally that by the time the season is over, we are quite ready to move on!)

This is one of my favourite soups. Roasting the asparagus gives the soup a much more intense flavour.

1 lb (500 g) asparagus, trimmed	1 cup chopped onions
2 tsp olive oil	1 cup diced Yukon Gold potatoes
Salt and freshly ground pepper	4 cups chicken stock
2 tbsp butter	$1/4$ cup whipping cream

PREHEAT oven to 450 F.

CUT asparagus into 1-inch lengths and set aside tips. Toss asparagus stalks with oil, salt and pepper and spread on a baking sheet. Roast for 4 to 8 minutes, or until asparagus is tender-crisp and slightly browned.

HEAT butter in a pot over medium heat while asparagus is roasting. Add onions and sauté for 4 minutes, or until translucent. Add roasted asparagus stalks, potatoes and stock. Bring to a boil, cover and simmer for 10 to 15 minutes, or until potatoes are soft.

ADD asparagus tips and cook for 3 minutes longer, or until tips are tender. Reserve a few tips for garnish.

PUREE soup and return to pot. Add cream and simmer for a few minutes. Taste and adjust seasonings. Serve garnished with asparagus tips.

Snow Pea Soup

SERVES 4

I have often made green pea soup, but I never thought to make snow pea soup until I tasted it in Vienna. It is beautiful and flavourful, perfect before a sophisticated main course or as a vegetarian starter. You could substitute sugar snaps, or use 3 cups regular green peas.

Frothing the soup before serving gives it a lighter texture and a modern look.

8 oz (250 g) snow peas	1 cup baby spinach
3 leeks, white and light-green part only, chopped	1 cup buttermilk
½ cup chopped Yukon Gold potatoes	Salt and freshly ground pepper
3 cups water	2 tbsp chopped chives

REMOVE strings from snow peas and cut peas into 1-inch pieces. Combine snow peas, leeks, potatoes and water in a pot and bring to a boil. Reduce heat and simmer gently for 10 minutes.

ADD spinach and simmer for 5 minutes longer, or until vegetables are soft.

PUREE soup with buttermilk and return to pot. Reheat and season well with salt and pepper.

FROTH soup using a milk frother or hand blender. Serve garnished with chives.

{ simmer or boil }

When a recipe calls for simmering, it means the food is cooked at a heat (technically 190 F) that produces small bubbles and movement in the liquid, but very little steam. When liquid is boiled (at 212 F), large bubbles form, and you can see steam.

{ buttermilk }

No buttermilk? Add 1 tsp lemon juice to 1 cup milk. The milk will curdle. Use in place of buttermilk.

Chili Squash Soup

SERVES 4

My e-mails at the *Globe and Mail* tell me that this soup is a big hit. Everyone loves the subtle spiciness and hint of orange.

2 tbsp butter	4 cups diced butternut squash
1 cup chopped onions	3 cups chicken stock
1 tsp ground coriander	½ cup orange juice
1 tsp ground cumin	Salt and freshly ground pepper
½ tsp ground fennel seeds	¼ cup sour cream
¼ tsp chili flakes	2 tbsp chopped chives
Pinch ground cloves	

HEAT butter in a large pot over medium heat. Add onions and sauté for about 2 minutes, or until softened.

STIR in coriander, cumin, fennel, chili flakes and cloves. Add squash and mix with spices.

ADD stock and orange juice and bring to a boil. Reduce heat and simmer until squash is soft, about 10 to 15 minutes.

PUREE soup and return to pot. Season with salt and pepper. Reheat and serve with a swirl of sour cream and chives.

{ squash }

The most popular
and readily available squashes are acorn and butternut, but when we ran a taste test of different squash varieties, they ended up at the bottom of the heap—bland and watery. They work well in soups (meatier varieties need more stock) and are convenient to use because they are often sold precut.

Far more interesting in both taste and texture are orange or green Hubbard squash and—the flavour winner—buttercup, a flattened, round, orange and green squash. These varieties have a meatier texture and enough taste that they are perfect enhanced with just a little salt, pepper and butter. They are great for roasting and for squash gratins.

Pumpkins are squash, too, but they are less flavourful than other squashes, unless you can find a really ripe one. I usually substitute Hubbard or buttercup squash in pumpkin pies.

Squash can be hard to cut. The secret is to give the stem a hard tap with the blunt edge of a knife to remove it. Once the stem has been removed, use a large knife to cut the squash in half.

Squash and Chanterelle Soup

SERVES 4 TO 6

Chanterelles are wonderful in this rich, flavourful soup, but they are out of season for half the year. Substitute thinly sliced oyster mushrooms.

1 small buttercup squash
2 tbsp olive oil
Salt and freshly ground pepper
1 cup chopped onions
1 tsp chopped garlic
Pinch cayenne

1 tsp chopped fresh thyme, or $1/4$ tsp dried
4 cups chicken stock
2 tbsp butter
2 oz (60 g) chanterelles, torn in half or quartered
    if large
2 tbsp whipping cream

PREHEAT oven to 400 F.

CUT squash into quarters and remove seeds. Place squash on a baking sheet skin side down. Brush flesh with 1 tbsp oil, season with salt and pepper and bake for 35 minutes, or until squash is golden and soft. Scoop out flesh.

HEAT remaining 1 tbsp oil in a pot over medium-high heat. Add onions, garlic and cayenne and sauté for 2 minutes, or until softened. Stir in thyme, reserved squash and stock and bring to a boil. Reduce heat and simmer for 10 minutes.

PREPARE mushrooms while soup is simmering by heating butter in a small skillet over medium-high heat. Add chanterelles and sauté for 3 minutes, or until softened and browned.

PUREE soup, return to pot and stir in cream. Add chanterelles to soup. Reheat and season well with salt and pepper.

Spiced Clam Chowder

SERVES 4

This is more like an Asian-spiced clam broth than a thick, creamy chowder. It is a superb first course, especially as a prelude to the rich flavour of lamb.

1 tbsp vegetable oil	18 fresh clams (in the shell)
1 ½ cups diced red potatoes	2 tbsp lime juice
1 ½ cups diced fennel	2 tbsp chopped fresh coriander
1 tsp Thai red curry paste	Salt and freshly ground pepper
4 cups chicken or fish stock	

HEAT oil in a pot over medium heat. Add potatoes and fennel and sauté for 2 minutes. Stir in curry paste and sauté for 1 minute.

ADD stock, bring to a boil, reduce heat and simmer for 10 minutes.

ADD clams and simmer until shells open, about 5 to 7 minutes. Discard any clams that haven't opened. Reserve 4 clams. Take remaining clams out of shells and return to pot along with any clam juices. Add lime juice and coriander and simmer for 1 more minute. Season with salt and pepper. Garnish each serving with a clam in the shell.

{ garnishing soups }

For an extra touch and special presentation, add a simple garnish to your soups.

- Chop up some of the blanched vegetable used to make the soup and sprinkle it on each serving. (This is always a good psychological move so people can recognize what kind of soup they are eating!)
- Sprinkle soup with chopped green onions or chives (include the purple flowers) or a little crumbled bacon.
- Homemade or storebought croutons can be sprinkled on top at the last minute.
- Add a dollop of sour cream or streak whipped cream on top of each serving. Swirl in a pattern for an interesting effect.
- Grate cheese on hot soup; it will melt into a delicious garnish.

Roasted Cauliflower Bisque

SERVES 4 TO 6

Roasting cauliflower heightens its taste in this luxurious, yummy soup. The cauliflower and caviar have a real affinity, but you can substitute chopped smoked salmon for the caviar if desired.

This soup is equally good served cold.

4 cups cauliflower florets (1- to 2-inch pieces)
1 tbsp olive oil
Salt and freshly ground pepper
4 or 5 sprigs fresh thyme
1 tbsp butter
2 cups chopped leeks (white and light-green
    part only)

4 cups chicken stock
$1/4$ cup whipping cream
1 tsp lemon juice
2 tbsp caviar, smoked salmon or chopped chives

PREHEAT oven to 450 F.

TOSS cauliflower in a large bowl with oil, salt, pepper and thyme and spread on a baking sheet. Bake for 15 to 20 minutes, or until golden, turning once during baking. Discard thyme.

HEAT butter in a pot over medium heat while cauliflower is roasting. Add leeks and sauté for about 3 minutes, or until limp. Add stock, bring to a boil and simmer for 5 minutes.

ADD roasted cauliflower to soup and simmer for 10 minutes, or until florets are soft.

PUREE soup until very smooth. Return to pot, add cream and lemon juice and reheat. Season if necessary. Top with caviar, smoked salmon or chives before serving.

Sweet Potato, Lemongrass and Ginger Soup

SERVES 4

Adding the whipping cream to this soup will make it more luxurious, but I also like the spiciness of the soup without the cream.

The soup is also excellent served hot.

1 tbsp butter	1 $\frac{1}{2}$ tsp finely chopped gingerroot
4 cups diced sweet potatoes	3 $\frac{1}{2}$ cups chicken stock
2 cups sliced leeks	$\frac{1}{4}$ cup whipping cream
1 tbsp finely chopped lemongrass	Salt and freshly ground pepper

HEAT butter in a pot over medium heat. Add sweet potatoes and leeks and cook for 5 minutes, or until potatoes are beginning to soften.

ADD lemongrass and ginger and cook for 1 minute, or until fragrant. Add stock, bring to a boil, reduce heat and simmer for 10 minutes, or until potatoes are very soft.

PUREE soup and stir in cream. Chill. Add salt and pepper to taste before serving.

{ serving cold soups }

Cold soups are a refreshing starter before a barbecue or simple summer meal. Serve the soup in chilled glass mugs or pottery bowls of a contrasting colour. Garnish with refreshing tidbits such as chopped gingerroot, slices of lime, or sprigs of fresh herbs. Or chill the bowl, paint the rim with a little egg white and press the rim into finely chopped fresh herbs.

Always taste and reseason cold soups before serving; some of the flavour will be lost in chilling.

{ salads }

House Salad

SERVES 4

Salads can be served as an appetizer, a main course or as a palate cleanser between courses at an elegant dinner. They can be full of eclectic flavours or focus on one or two succulent ingredients. Salad making is an art, and a well-made salad is lively, palate pleasing and beautiful to look at.

This is the salad that we have nearly every night at home. Out of laziness and a desire not to wash and dry lettuce, I buy organic spring mix, which I beef up with torn escarole, sliced Belgian endive, chopped red onions and croutons.

4 cups spring or mesclun mix
1/2 head escarole, torn
1 Belgian endive, sliced
1/2 cup chopped red onions
1/2 cup croutons

House Dressing
1 tbsp white wine vinegar
1 tbsp balsamic vinegar
1/3 cup olive oil
Salt and freshly ground pepper

COMBINE spring mix, escarole and Belgian endive in a bowl. Sprinkle with red onions.

WHISK wine vinegar and balsamic vinegar in a bowl. Whisk in oil until well combined. Season well with salt and pepper.

TOSS salad with dressing. Add croutons.

{ croutons }

Challah is egg bread, and it makes light but crisp croutons.

In a large bowl, combine 1/3 cup olive oil with 1 tbsp finely chopped garlic. Cut challah into 1/2-inch slices and remove crusts. Cut bread into cubes. Toss bread cubes with oil mixture and season with salt.

Spread croutons on a baking sheet and bake in a preheated 350 F oven for 5 minutes. Turn and bake for 5 to 8 minutes longer, or until croutons are light brown. Store in an airtight container at room temperature for up to a month.

Makes 6 cups.

There are many mixes of baby lettuces—some organic, others not. The mix varies, but generally three to eight varieties are included.

Mesclun is the Provençal name for a mix that usually includes arugula, mache, oakleaf, frisee, radicchio and baby Romaine. Often a few herbs such as chervil and Italian parsley are added to the mixes.

Spirited Dressing

MAKES 1 CUP

This lively dressing is excellent with strongly flavoured salads made with greens such as escarole, frisee and watercress, as well as cooked vegetable salads.

1 tbsp finely chopped shallots	1 tbsp grainy mustard
1 tbsp finely chopped red onions	1/2 cup olive oil
1 tsp minced garlic	Salt and freshly ground pepper
1/4 cup red wine vinegar	2 tbsp chopped parsley

WHISK shallots, onions, garlic, vinegar and mustard in a bowl. Slowly whisk in oil.

SEASON with salt and pepper and stir in parsley.

Miso Ginger Vinaigrette

MAKES 1/2 CUP

Serve this low-fat, low-calorie vinaigrette over salad greens, cooked or raw spinach, sliced cucumber, steamed broccoli, asparagus or cauliflower. If it seems too thick, whisk in a little water.

1/4 cup light miso	1 tsp granulated sugar
1/4 cup rice vinegar	1/2 tsp sesame oil
1 tbsp grated gingerroot	Dash hot pepper sauce

WHISK miso, vinegar, ginger, sugar, sesame oil and hot pepper sauce in a bowl until combined.

Vinaigrettes

Vinaigrettes are a combination of oil, vinegar, herbs and spices. They can be used on an assortment of dishes, from salads to vegetable dishes and meats.

Oils carry the flavour of the vinaigrette. Use good-quality olive oil or vegetable oils such as canola or safflower. I always use extra-virgin olive oil for salads because I like its distinct peppery flavour. Taste different brands until you find one you really like. For a change, try nut oils such as hazelnut or walnut; they combine well with fruit vinegars and are at their best on plain green salads that do not fight with their flavour.

The sharp taste of vinegar cuts through the oil, balancing the vinaigrette. Any vinegar can be used in a salad dressing, but some are better than others. I find plain white vinegar too tart and acidic, so the less acidic red and white wine vinegars are the mainstays of my salad dressings. White wine vinegar creates a pale, creamy vinaigrette; red a more rosy-hued one.

Other acids such as lemon or lime juice can be used instead of vinegar. Use three parts oil to one part acid for the best results.

In vinaigrettes the oil and vinegar can be emulsified to form a creamy dressing. But oil and vinegar will not form an emulsion on their own. Dijon mustard helps to emulsify a dressing, as well as adding a little spiciness. Mayonnaise can also act as the emulsifier.

To emulsify the dressing, always beat the emulsifier into the seasonings and vinegar before slowly whisking in the oil. If your dressing tastes too oily, add salt to help eliminate the oily taste.

Don't add too much vinaigrette to salads. They will lose their freshness and become wilted. Use about $1/3$ cup dressing for 6 cups lettuce. (Remember that although salads are low calorie, salad dressings are not.)

Make the dressing in quantity and store it in the refrigerator for up to a month. It's healthier, cheaper and better-tasting than storebought dressing.

Spring Salad

SERVES 4

I first discovered wild leeks during a spring walk in the forest. I dug up the plants and tried to transplant them into my garden at home, to no avail. I learned that wild plants generally do not take well to a tame environment, which makes them a rare delicacy indeed. Wild leeks are only available in the spring, so if they are unavailable, use the white parts of regular leeks. Slice them very thinly and blanch in boiling water for 1 minute before using.

Use the leftover cooked egg whites as a garnish for cooked asparagus or other green salads.

2 bunches wild leeks, trimmed, or 2 cups thinly
    sliced regular leeks, blanched
4 cups mache
1 tbsp sherry vinegar

$1/4$ cup olive oil
Salt and freshly ground pepper
2 hard-boiled egg yolks

CHOP stems of wild leeks, leaving leaves whole. Combine leeks and mache in a bowl.

WHISK sherry vinegar, oil, salt and pepper in a bowl.

TOSS salad with dressing. Grate hard-boiled egg yolks over salad. Taste and adjust seasonings if necessary.

{ hard-boiling eggs }

For perfect hard-boiled eggs, place eggs in a pot of cold, salted water and bring to a boil. Boil for 2 minutes, remove pot from heat, cover and let sit for 10 minutes. Drain and run under cold water.

{ mache }

Also known as lamb's quarters, corn salad or field salad, mache grows in delicate clumps and has spoon-shaped leaves. Remove the little roots before using. It has a distinctive nutty, buttery flavour and is good by itself or combined with other mild lettuces.

{ wild leeks }

Wild leeks are easily recognized by their tulip-like leaves, purplish stems and small onion-like bulbs. They have a strong smell and deliver lots of flavour for such fragile-looking greens. Their taste is garlicky and onion-like at the same time.

Winter Salad

SERVES 4

This recipe makes twice the amount of dressing that you need, but it is a great creamy oil-free, low-calorie dressing to have on hand, and it keeps for about a week in the refrigerator.

Use your favourite winter lettuces in this salad.

4 cups watercress or torn escarole

1 cup torn radicchio

1 Belgian endive, sliced

1/2 cup chopped red onions

Low-Fat Dill and Garlic Dressing

1/2 tsp minced garlic

1/2 cup light sour cream

1/4 cup buttermilk

2 tbsp lemon juice

2 tbsp chopped fresh dill

Salt and fresh ground pepper

COMBINE watercress, radicchio, Belgian endive and onions in a bowl.

WHISK garlic, sour cream, buttermilk, lemon juice, dill, salt and pepper in a bowl. Taste and adjust seasonings, adding lemon juice and dill if necessary.

TOSS greens with about 1/2 cup dressing.

{ belgian endive }

Elongated and elegant, Belgian endive is grown in dark storage rooms to keep it white. Its slight bitterness makes it a good match with other assertive lettuces such as radicchio and watercress. It becomes sweet when cooked, especially braised in a little stock with a bit of butter and sugar. It is grown from the chicory root—originally grown to be roasted and ground as a coffee substitute.

Strawberry, Macadamia Nut and Spinach Salad

SERVES 8

The combination of macadamia nuts, strawberries, spinach and honey makes an unusual but splendid early-summer salad.

½ English cucumber, peeled and diced	**Honey Mustard Vinaigrette**
Salt to taste	2 tsp honey
4 cups strawberries, hulled and halved	1 tbsp grainy mustard
8 cups baby spinach	2 tbsp sherry vinegar
¼ cup chervil or parsley sprigs	½ cup olive oil
⅔ cup macadamia nuts	Salt and freshly ground pepper

SALT cucumber lightly and let drain in a colander for 30 minutes to allow juices to drip out. Pat cucumber dry with paper towels.

TOSS cucumber, strawberries, spinach, chervil and macadamia nuts in a large bowl.

PREPARE dressing by whisking honey, mustard and vinegar in a bowl. Slowly whisk in oil and season with salt and pepper.

TOSS salad with dressing.

{ salting vegetables }

Vegetables such as cabbage, fennel, onion and cucumber are sometimes salted to remove some of their water if they are going to be eaten raw. Salting also makes them softer and more digestible. Regular eggplant is salted to remove the bitter juices that can interfere with its taste (Japanese, Italian and Sicilian eggplants do not need to be salted).

Heirloom Tomato and Mozzarella Salad

SERVES 4

Buffalo mozzarella is a soft, creamy cheese sold in large brine-covered balls. You could substitute bocconcini—regular mozzarella sold in little balls—but I think it has about as much flavour as a tennis ball, so if I can't find buffalo mozzarella, I look for fresh mozzarella or I leave out the cheese and serve this as a plain tomato salad.

2 large heirloom or other tomatoes	3 tbsp olive oil
1 large ball buffalo mozzarella	1 tbsp balsamic vinegar
8 large basil leaves	Salt to taste

CUT tomatoes and mozzarella into slices about ½ inch thick and arrange on individual salad plates, tucking basil leaves between slices.

DRIZZLE with oil and balsamic vinegar and sprinkle with salt.

{ heirloom tomatoes }

Heirloom tomatoes are old varieties that have been handed down through generations by seed saving. They have not been genetically modified and are usually grown organically. You'll find them in season at farmers' markets and in high-end grocery stores. There are many varieties, including dark purple Brandywines and the green-striped Zebra tomatoes. They are often odd shaped and odd coloured (some are even green when they're ripe), but their taste and juiciness are unsurpassed. Serve them simply in summer salads.

{ buffalo mozzarella }

Fresh buffalo milk mozzarella has an outstanding slightly nutty taste with a tinge of salt. The texture is soft and crumbly, not rubbery. It is made from buffalo milk and generally imported from Italy. Substitute freshly made mozzarella, called "fior de latte," not the drier, more aged kind.

Roasted Asparagus, Chive and Asiago Salad

SERVES 8

This is a simple but excellent salad to serve with chicken or fish. Roasting the asparagus brings out all its flavour.

2 lb (1 kg) asparagus	**White Wine Vinaigrette**
2 tbsp olive oil	1 tbsp white wine vinegar
Salt and freshly ground pepper	1 tsp lemon juice
1/2 cup chives (cut in 3-inch lengths)	1/4 cup olive oil
4 oz (125 g) Asiago cheese	Salt and freshly ground pepper

PREHEAT oven to 450 F.

SNAP bottom ends off asparagus. If stalks are thick, peel with a vegetable peeler. Place on an oiled baking sheet and brush with oil. Season with salt and pepper.

ROAST asparagus for 4 to 8 minutes, depending on thickness, until tender-crisp. Cool. Toss with chives in a bowl.

SHAVE Asiago cheese with a vegetable peeler. Reserve.

PREPARE dressing by whisking vinegar and lemon juice in a bowl. Whisk in oil. Season well with salt and pepper.

TOSS asparagus with dressing and garnish with cheese.

{ asparagus }

Snap the woody ends off asparagus stalks, as they are usually dry. Thick stalks of asparagus should be peeled, but thin stalks can be left as is. Using a vegetable peeler, peel stalks from the head to the base.

{ wine vinegars }

Wine vinegars are becoming the next big trend. The quality depends on the quality of the wine or grapes, so the range is enormous. The best vinegars taste of the wine they are made from. California and Spain both make excellent products, and now Canada is beginning to produce good wine vinegars as well.

Look for a vinegar that suits your taste. Some are stronger and more flavourful than others. Add a touch of sugar to your dressing if the vinegar is too tart.

Roquefort, Walnut and Grape Salad

SERVES 4

Use good-quality extra-virgin olive oil in this dressing—it makes a real difference. If sherry vinegar is unavailable, substitute red wine vinegar.

1 Belgian endive, sliced

1 small head radicchio, torn

1 small bunch arugula, trimmed and torn

1 cup crumbled Roquefort cheese

1 cup toasted walnuts

$\frac{1}{2}$ cup red seedless grapes, halved

1 tbsp sherry vinegar

$\frac{1}{4}$ cup olive oil

Salt and freshly ground pepper

COMBINE Belgian endive, radicchio and arugula in a bowl. Sprinkle on cheese, walnuts and grapes and toss.

WHISK vinegar, oil, salt and pepper in a bowl. Toss salad with dressing.

{ toasting nuts and spices }

Toasting nuts and spices before using will make them more flavourful.

To toast nuts, place them on a parchment-lined baking sheet and bake in a preheated 350 F oven for 8 to 10 minutes, or until golden. To toast spices, place them in a dry skillet over low heat and cook, stirring frequently, until you can smell the spices. Remove from the skillet immediately.

{ sherry vinegar }

Spain has been making sherry vinegar for at least five hundred years. Originally appearing by accident when the sherry was being made—to the great distress of the winery owners—sherry vinegar is now the result of a highly refined process and painstaking effort. It is regarded by many as the finest of vinegars.

Traditionally, sherry vinegars are aged for thirty to seventy-five years, and high-quality versions are more expensive than sherry itself. It is a sweet vinegar with a sharp, sour after-taste and is excellent in sauces and salads.

Asparagus, Spinach and Fennel Salad

SERVES 6

This salad brims with freshness and snap. If you can't find fennel, use Belgian endive instead.

To turn this into a more substantial dish, drape smoked salmon or prosciutto over the finished salad or add slices of slivered Parmigiano Reggiano or Spanish Manchego cheese.

The tarragon dressing is my all-time favourite; I like the creaminess as well as the spring-like, licorice taste.

1 small bulb fennel, trimmed	**Creamy Tarragon Dressing**
Salt	2 tbsp mayonnaise
8 oz (250 g) asparagus, trimmed	2 tbsp white wine vinegar
6 cups baby spinach	1 tsp chopped fresh tarragon, or $1/4$ tsp dried
	$1/4$ tsp minced garlic
	$1/3$ cup olive oil
	Salt and freshly ground pepper

CUT fennel in half and remove core. Using a mandoline or a sharp knife, slice fennel thinly. Place in a bowl, sprinkle with salt and let sit for 30 minutes.

BRING a large skillet of salted water to a boil. Add asparagus and boil for 2 minutes, or until tender-crisp. Drain and refresh under cold water until cold and pat dry. Cut stalks into 2-inch pieces.

COMBINE asparagus and spinach in a bowl.

PREPARE dressing by whisking mayonnaise, vinegar, tarragon and garlic in a bowl. Slowly whisk in oil. Season well with salt and pepper.

PAT fennel dry and add to asparagus. Toss salad with dressing.

{ mandoline }

A mandoline is a hand-held kitchen tool that can slice, shred, julienne and waffle-cut vegetables or fruit. Different blades can be attached and adjusted for thickness.

The French make fine chef-quality mandolines, but the Japanese versions are also excellent and much less expensive.

Arugula Salad with Goat Cheese and Pesto

SERVES 4

A simple salad with complex tastes. Use homemade or storebought pesto.

Buy a firm goat cheese (the kind that comes with a rind); Quebec is producing very good and interesting goat cheeses that would work well in this recipe.

1 large bunch arugula	6 oz (175 g) firm goat cheese
2 tbsp olive oil	¼ cup pesto
1 tbsp balsamic vinegar	¼ cup toasted pine nuts
Salt and freshly ground pepper	

TRIM arugula and toss in a large bowl with oil and balsamic vinegar. Sprinkle with salt and pepper.

DIVIDE arugula among individual serving plates. Cut goat cheese into 4 pieces and place on arugula. Top each serving with a tablespoon of pesto and sprinkle with pine nuts.

{ pesto }

Combine 2 garlic cloves, 2 tbsp pine nuts, 2 cups fresh basil (packed) and ½ cup olive oil. Process until smooth. Season with salt and freshly ground pepper to taste (pesto can be frozen at this point).

Before using, stir in ¼ cup grated Parmesan cheese and 2 tbsp additional olive oil. Makes about 1½ cups.

{ arugula }

Arugula is my favourite lettuce—peppery and nutty in flavour, with oak-leaf-shaped leaves. I use it in everything. It is excellent as a garnish for a main course as well as mixed with other greens in a salad. Arugula is also known as rocket or rucola.

Creamy Brie Salad with Apples

SERVES 4

Garnish this salad with edible flowers, if desired. The elegantly flavoured dressing is not very tart, making it a good match with the Brie. Serve this as a cheese course, if desired.

1 bunch arugula, trimmed	**Apple Cider Mustard Vinaigrette**
1 small head radicchio	$\frac{1}{2}$ tsp honey mustard
$\frac{1}{2}$ cup dried apple slices, halved	2 tbsp apple cider
6 oz (175 g) ripe Brie	2 tbsp cider vinegar
	1 tbsp finely chopped shallots
	$\frac{1}{3}$ cup olive oil
	Salt and freshly ground pepper

TEAR arugula and radicchio into small pieces and combine in a bowl. Sprinkle with dried apples.

CUT Brie into 4 wedges and arrange on individual plates.

WHISK mustard, cider, vinegar and shallots in a bowl. Slowly whisk in oil. Season with salt and pepper.

TOSS lettuce with dressing and place a portion of salad beside each piece of Brie.

{ handling lettuce }

Choose lettuce that has no blemishes, brown spots or wilted leaves. Look for a fresh green or red colour.

Wash your lettuce in lots of water. Spin dry with a salad spinner, wrap in paper towels and store in a plastic bag for up to a week in the refrigerator. Organic baby lettuce mixes are prewashed; store them in a sealed bag with a dry paper towel.

Instead of chopping lettuce, tear the leaves into chunks or leave whole if they are small. Dress salads just before serving to prevent them from becoming limp. (If I am preparing a salad ahead of time for a dinner party, I put the dressing in the bowl with the leaves on top and then toss the salad just before serving.)

Guacamole Salad

SERVES 4

An interesting, tasty and unusual salad that uses the ingredients for guacamole in a very different manner. The red-tinged dressing is fresh, herbal and slightly spicy. It is also excellent on corn salads.

4 plum tomatoes
1 tbsp olive oil
Salt and freshly ground pepper
1 jalapeño, halved and seeded
4 cups torn escarole
2 avocadoes, peeled and diced
½ cup diced red onions

Navajo Dressing
¼ cup chopped roasted red pepper
1 tsp minced garlic
2 tbsp lime juice
1 ½ tsp granulated sugar
Hot pepper sauce to taste
¼ cup olive oil

Garnish
2 tbsp chopped fresh coriander

PREHEAT oven to 350 F.

CUT tomatoes in half and remove seeds. Place cut side up on an oiled baking sheet. Brush with oil and sprinkle with salt and pepper.

ROAST tomatoes for 30 minutes. Add jalapeño to baking sheet and continue to roast jalapeño and tomatoes for 30 minutes, or until browned and semi-dried. Dice tomatoes and jalapeño. Reserve jalapeño for dressing.

TOSS escarole, avocadoes, onions and tomatoes in a large bowl or platter.

COMBINE red pepper, jalapeño, garlic, lime juice, sugar, hot pepper sauce and oil in a food processor or blender. Process until smooth.

TOSS salad with dressing and sprinkle with coriander.

{ escarole }

Escarole is pale green and slightly bitter. It is part of the chicory family. Mix it with frisee and other chicories and combine with assertive ingredients such as blue cheese, nuts and bacon. It is also good stir-fried.

James's Winter Greek Salad

SERVES 6

Pick up storebought cooked beets for this dish, or wrap whole beets in foil and bake at 350 F for an hour before peeling and slicing.

This recipe comes from my friend James Chatto, who lives part time in Corfu. He always uses Greek feta in this salad (it is creamier and less salty than other varieties), but if you prefer a stronger flavour, try Bulgarian feta.

1 head Romaine lettuce	1 tbsp chopped fresh dill
1 cup diced feta cheese	Salt and freshly ground pepper
$1/2$ cup sliced red onions	$1/4$ cup olive oil
$1 1/2$ cups diced cooked beets	2 tbsp red wine vinegar
1 cup pitted Kalamata olives	

TEAR lettuce into bite-sized pieces and scatter over a platter. Add feta, onions, beets and olives in layers.

SPRINKLE salad with dill and season with salt and pepper.

SPRINKLE oil and vinegar over salad. Toss just before serving.

White Bean Salad

SERVES 4

A fresh-tasting last-minute salad that is excellent with chicken or fish.

1 19-oz (540 mL) can cannellini or white kidney
   beans, rinsed and drained
1 cup diced English cucumber
½ cup chopped green onions
1 cup chopped fennel or celery

Lemon Mint Vinaigrette
3 tbsp lemon juice
2 tsp Dijon mustard
½ tsp minced garlic
½ cup olive oil
1 tsp grated lemon rind
3 tbsp chopped fresh mint
Salt and freshly ground pepper

COMBINE beans, cucumber, green onions and fennel in a large bowl.

PREPARE dressing by whisking lemon juice, mustard and garlic in a small bowl. Slowly whisk in oil. Stir in lemon rind and mint. Season with salt and pepper.

TOSS beans and vegetables gently with dressing.

Chickpea and Cucumber Salad

SERVES 8

A refreshing, subtly spiced salad to serve with curry or Asian chicken and rice. A good salad for the buffet table.

2 19-oz (540 mL) cans chickpeas, rinsed and
   drained
1 tsp chopped jalapeño
1 English cucumber, diced
1 cup diced red onions
½ cup chopped fresh coriander

½ cup plain yogurt
1 tsp grated lime rind
1 tbsp lime juice
1 tbsp cumin seeds
Salt and freshly ground pepper

COMBINE chickpeas, jalapeño, cucumber, onions, coriander, yogurt, lime rind, lime juice and cumin in a bowl. Season with salt and pepper.

Israeli Salad

SERVES 6

In Israel, this salad is served with everything from breakfast to dinner. There are similar versions in all Eastern European countries. It is best eaten the day it is made. Add feta if desired.

1 English cucumber, peeled and diced	4 radishes, cut in wedges
2 large tomatoes, seeded and diced	Salt and freshly ground pepper
1 yellow pepper, seeded and diced	$\frac{1}{4}$ cup lemon juice
4 green onions, cut in $\frac{1}{2}$-inch lengths	$\frac{1}{4}$ cup olive oil

COMBINE cucumber, tomatoes, yellow pepper, green onions and radishes in a bowl. Sprinkle with salt and pepper.

WHISK lemon juice and oil in a small bowl. Toss vegetables with dressing.

Potato, Green Bean and Tomato Salad

SERVES 6

This outstanding colourful, easy salad could be served on a buffet or at a barbecue. Oakleaf, Bibb, Boston or mixed soft lettuces are best in this mix. Garnish it with extra chives and fresh tarragon sprigs.

Creamy Herb Dressing	Salad
¼ cup white wine vinegar	1 lb (500 g) small red potatoes, halved
2 tbsp chopped chives	2 tbsp olive oil
1 tbsp chopped fresh tarragon	Salt and freshly ground pepper
1 tbsp chopped parsley	6 oz (175 g) green beans, trimmed and halved
¼ cup olive oil	½ cup yellow cherry tomatoes
¼ cup whipping cream	½ cup red cherry tomatoes
Salt and freshly ground pepper	1 cup chopped red onions
	⅓ cup pitted black olives, halved
	Oakleaf or other lettuce

PREHEAT oven to 400 F.

WHISK vinegar, chives, tarragon and parsley in a bowl. Slowly whisk in oil and cream. Season with salt and pepper.

TOSS potatoes with oil, salt and pepper. Place cut side down on a baking sheet and roast for 25 to 40 minutes (depending on size of potatoes), or until tender. Transfer to a large bowl and toss with half the dressing.

BRING a pot of salted water to a boil while potatoes are roasting. Add green beans and boil for 3 minutes, or until tender-crisp. Refresh with cold water until cool and drain well. Add to potatoes. Stir in half the remaining dressing.

CUT cherry tomatoes in half and add to salad. Stir in red onions and olives. Toss with remaining dressing and taste and adjust seasonings if necessary.

LINE a platter with lettuce and place salad on top.

{ oakleaf lettuce }

Part of the loose-leaf lettuce group that includes Bibb and Boston, oakleaf has deeply indented, tender leaves that look like oak leaves. The stems are crunchy. It comes in red and green varieties and is excellent in a mixed salad or by itself.

{ fish and seafood }

Miso Black Cod

SERVES 4

Fish is one of the bases of healthy, fast cooking. It contains heart-healthy Omega-3 oils (especially abundant in fatty fish), and is quick and easy to prepare.

Miso cod is featured in many fusion and Japanese restaurants. For the right taste and texture, the cod should be marinated for at least 24 hours (or up to three days for maximum flavour).

This is based on a recipe from Tojo, the famous Japanese sushi chef in Vancouver.

4 Alaskan black cod fillets (about 6 oz/175 g each), skin on	1 tbsp granulated sugar
	1 tsp finely chopped gingerroot
Salt	1 cup enoki mushrooms
1 cup light miso	2 tbsp olive oil
¼ cup sake	6 cups baby spinach
¼ cup mirin	1 tbsp seasoned rice vinegar

SPRINKLE cod lightly with salt and let sit for 1 hour. Wipe off salt with a paper towel.

COMBINE miso, sake, mirin, sugar and ginger in a large bowl or deep baking dish. Add cod and spoon over marinade so cod is fully covered. Cover and marinate for at least 24 hours, refrigerated.

PREHEAT oven to 350 F.

PLACE enoki mushrooms on a baking sheet and bake for 10 minutes to remove any moisture.

HEAT 1 tbsp oil in a large ovenproof skillet over high heat. Scrape marinade from cod and place fish skin side down in skillet. Sear for 1 minute, then place skillet in oven for 8 to 10 minutes, or until fish is just cooked.

TOSS mushrooms, spinach, vinegar and remaining 1 tbsp oil in a large bowl. Place on plates and top with cod.

{ mirin }

Mirin is a golden-hued, sweet, low-alcohol Japanese cooking wine made from glutinous rice. It is available at the supermarket. Sake is a high-alcohol fermented rice wine used both in cooking and for drinking. Serve it chilled (only cheap sake is served warm).

Know your fishmonger. If you trust the store where you buy your fish, you should not have to worry about freshness, but here are some ways to tell whether fish is fresh.

Look for fish with a clear eye. A cloudy or sunken eye means the fish is not fresh.

If you press the fish with your finger, the indentation should spring right back. If the flesh feels spongy, don't buy it.

Look under the gills; they should be bright red. If they are pink or brownish, the fish has been out of the water too long.

Fish should always smell fresh; it should never have a "fishy" odour.

With fish fillets it's harder to judge freshness, but the fillets should look translucent and feel firm to the touch. If you are buying fish steaks, select centre-cut steaks. They are more tender than the cuts from the tail.

Some firmer-fleshed varieties, such as halibut, freeze well. Always defrost fish in the refrigerator overnight (rather than at room temperature or in the microwave) to reduce the loss of natural moisture.

Store fish for no more than a day or two, as it spoils quickly. Remove any plastic wrap and place the fish in a dish. Cover with a paper towel and store in the coldest part of your refrigerator. Rubbing fish with soy sauce or yogurt helps to preserve it, and it should last a little longer.

As fish consumption climbs and huge fishing fleets invade large patches of ocean, some species are disappearing. I personally would not buy Chilean sea bass, certain cod and tuna, or swordfish until the stocks rise again.

Roasted Halibut with Mustard Crumb Crust

SERVES 4

In this savoury dish, the vegetables are oven-roasted and then topped with crisp-crumbed halibut and returned to the oven for a brief time. Serve it with new potatoes and a salad for a special dinner. If you can find yellow zucchini, use two green and one yellow.

3 medium zucchini	1 tbsp soy sauce
2 red onions, peeled	2 tbsp butter
4 plum tomatoes	2 tsp finely chopped garlic
3 tbsp olive oil	1 cup fresh breadcrumbs
2 tsp chopped fresh thyme, or $\frac{1}{2}$ tsp dried	2 tbsp chopped parsley
1 tsp grated lemon rind	Salt and freshly ground pepper
1 tbsp Dijon mustard	4 halibut fillets (about 6 oz/175 g each),
1 tbsp grainy mustard	skin removed

PREHEAT oven to 450 F.

CUT zucchini into 1-inch chunks. Cut each onion into 6 wedges through the root. Cut tomatoes into quarters.

TOSS vegetables with 2 tbsp oil and 1 tsp thyme and spread in a baking dish in a single layer. Roast for 15 minutes, or until softened. Stir once during roasting.

PREPARE fish while vegetables are roasting. Combine remaining 1 tbsp oil, remaining 1 tsp thyme, lemon rind, mustards and soy sauce in a bowl. Reserve.

HEAT butter in a small skillet over medium heat. Add garlic and sauté for 1 minute. Stir in breadcrumbs and cook for 2 minutes, or just until breadcrumbs begin to colour. Stir in parsley and season with salt and pepper.

SEASON halibut with salt and pepper and brush mustard mixture on fish. Pat breadcrumb mixture on top of fish.

PLACE halibut on top of cooked vegetables and return to oven. Bake for 10 to 15 minutes, or until white juices just appear. Serve halibut with vegetables and any pan juices.

Braised Halibut with White Wine Sauce and Mussels

SERVES 4

The richness of this dish is balanced by the saltiness of the mussels and the fragrance of the coriander. To grind coriander seeds, place them in a pepper grinder or spice mill and grind coarsely.

4 halibut fillets (about 6 oz/175 g each),
    skin removed
Salt
1 tsp coarsely ground pepper
1 tsp coarsely ground coriander seeds
1/2 cup finely chopped shallots

1 cup white wine
20 mussels
1 tbsp whipping cream
1/2 cup butter, cold
2 tbsp chopped chives

PREHEAT oven to 450 F.

SEASON halibut with salt, pepper and coriander seeds.

SPREAD shallots over bottom of a baking dish and top with fish in a single layer. Pour wine around fish.

BAKE for 5 minutes. Add mussels and bake for 5 to 7 minutes longer, or until fish is just cooked and mussels open. Discard any mussels that haven't opened.

DRAIN liquid from baking dish into a skillet. Remove all but 8 mussels from shells and reserve shelled mussels. Cover halibut and mussels in shells with a tea towel to keep warm.

PLACE skillet over high heat and reduce liquid for 4 to 6 minutes, or until 2 tbsp remains. Reduce heat to low and add cream. Slowly whisk in butter 2 tbsp at a time. If sauce starts to separate, remove pan from heat. Sauce should thicken.

ADD shelled mussels and chives to skillet and season with pepper. Spoon sauce over fish and mussels in shell.

Grouper with Corn and Edamame

SERVES 4

Serve this with rice and a tomato salad. You can use halibut or Alaskan black cod instead of the grouper. For a lighter dish, use stock instead of whipping cream.

2 tbsp butter	1 ¼ cups shelled edamame
1 cup chopped red onions	½ cup fish or chicken stock
1 tsp finely chopped garlic	¼ cup whipping cream
1 ½ cups chopped red peppers	¼ cup soft goat cheese
1 tsp chopped jalapeño, optional	4 grouper fillets (about 6 oz/175 g each), skin on
1 ½ cups fresh or frozen corn kernels	Salt and freshly ground pepper

HEAT butter in a large skillet over medium high heat. Add onions, garlic, red peppers and jalapeño. Sauté for 2 minutes, or until softened.

ADD corn and continue to sauté until corn is tender and slightly browned, about 3 minutes longer.

STIR in edamame and cook for 2 minutes, or until hot.

ADD stock, cream and goat cheese and bring to a boil.

SEASON grouper with salt and pepper and place on vegetables. Cover skillet, reduce heat to low and cook for 7 to 8 minutes, or until grouper exudes some juice. Serve fish on vegetables and spoon sauce over top.

{ edamame }

Edamame are Japanese soybeans. They are available frozen, sold in their pods or shelled (a 1-lb bag of frozen edamame in the shell yields about 1 ¼ cups shelled edamame). Blanch the pods in boiling water for a few minutes. Refresh with cold water, then shell.

Wasabi-crusted Sole with Glazed Endive

SERVES 4

The heat of the unusual wasabi crust is balanced by the sweetness of the cooked endive, making an interesting combination for a light summer meal. Buy the snack package of wasabi peas for this. This coating is also good on boneless chicken breasts.

1 ½ cups dried wasabi peas	½ cup chicken stock
1 egg	¼ cup orange juice
Salt and freshly ground pepper	1 tsp grated lemon rind
1 ½ lb (750 g) sole fillets	2 tbsp vegetable oil
2 tbsp butter	2 tbsp chopped fresh coriander or parsley
2 tsp granulated sugar	Lemon wedges
4 Belgian endives, halved lengthwise	

GRIND peas in a food processor as finely as possible (there will be some texture left). Place on a plate. Beat egg with a pinch of salt in a shallow dish.

DIP fish into egg mixture, then press into wasabi powder to coat well.

HEAT butter in a large skillet over medium heat. Sprinkle in sugar and stir to dissolve. Add endives and cook for 5 minutes, turning occasionally, or until golden.

COMBINE stock, orange juice and lemon rind in a small bowl. Pour over endives, bring to a boil, cover, reduce heat and simmer until endives are soft when pierced with a knife, about 6 to 8 minutes.

REMOVE endives from skillet. Increase heat and reduce liquid in skillet for 2 minutes, or until it forms a glaze. Return endives to skillet, season with salt and pepper and keep warm.

HEAT oil in another large skillet over medium heat and fry fillets (in batches, if necessary), for about 1 to 2 minutes per side, or until cooked and golden. Add more oil if needed.

SERVE fillets accompanied by glazed endive. Sprinkle with coriander and garnish with lemon wedges.

{ sole }

Sole is a flat fish that belongs to the flounder family. The thinner, smaller fillets of grey or lemon sole are more delicate and tasty than the large fillets, but they can be used interchangeably. Dover sole is unfilleted grey sole and is usually cooked whole.

Striped Bass with Pesto

This quick Italian-based fish dish is perfect served with a side of pasta or risotto. Use home-made or storebought pesto. Substitute halibut or Alaskan black cod for the bass.

3 tbsp olive oil	1 tbsp chopped parsley
2 leeks, white and light-green part only, sliced	Salt and freshly ground pepper
1 clove garlic, slivered	$\frac{1}{4}$ cup pesto
$\frac{1}{4}$ cup white wine	$\frac{1}{2}$ cup fresh breadcrumbs
1 cup drained canned tomatoes, or 4 fresh tomatoes, chopped	4 striped bass fillets (about 6 oz/175 g each), skin on
$\frac{1}{4}$ cup pitted black olives	

PREHEAT oven to 350 F.

HEAT oil in a large skillet over medium-high heat. Add leeks and garlic and sauté for 4 minutes, or until leeks soften.

STIR in wine and tomatoes and cook for 10 minutes. Stir in olives and parsley and cook for 5 minutes longer, or until sauce thickens. Season with salt and pepper.

SPREAD sauce over base of a baking dish large enough to hold fillets in one layer. Top sauce with fillets (skin side down). Combine pesto and breadcrumbs in a small bowl and spread over fish. Bake for 25 to 35 minutes, or until white juices rise on fish.

{ striped bass }

Striped bass live in coastal ocean waters but spawn in fresh water. Farmed striped bass is a hybrid of white bass and wild striped bass, and it is less sweet than the wild version. Farmed bass have broken stripes and wild bass have solid stripes.

Fish Baked in Banana Leaves

SERVES 4

Banana leaves are available frozen in South Asian and Latin American grocery stores. They lend an exotic look and flavour to this dish but can be easily replaced with foil.

$\frac{1}{3}$ cup coconut milk

2 tbsp desiccated unsweetened coconut

$\frac{1}{4}$ cup chopped fresh coriander

2 tsp chopped gingerroot

1 tsp chopped green chili or hot Asian chili sauce

$\frac{1}{4}$ cup chopped green onions

4 banana leaves, defrosted

4 striped bass or red snapper fillets (about 6 oz/ 175 g each), skin on

PREHEAT oven to 450 F.

COMBINE coconut milk, coconut, coriander, ginger, chili and green onions in a food processor and process until fairly smooth.

PLACE banana leaves or foil on counter. Place a fish fillet, skin side down, in centre of each leaf. Spoon marinade over fish. Enclose fish in leaves, making sure there are no open edges. Tie banana leaves with string, or seal foil.

PLACE banana leaves on a baking sheet and bake for 10 minutes. Remove from oven and let cool for 2 minutes. Unwrap fish and place banana leaves, fish and its juices on plates.

{ coconut milk }

Look for cans that list coconut milk as the first ingredient (some brands are mostly water). Shake well before using.

Coconut milk is highly perishable and does not stay fresh for longer than two or three days, so freeze any extra in a plastic container.

Macadamia-crusted Mahi Mahi with Tropical Salsa

SERVES 4

I had this dish in Hawaii, where fish is often served with a fruity side dish. The recipe also works well with boneless, skinless chicken breasts (though they will take longer to cook).

Mahi mahi is a mild fish best served with a sweet hot salsa like this one. If you wish, streak each plate with additional Asian chili sauce for some extra fire. Use leftover fruit in a fruit salad.

Tropical Salsa	Fish
½ cup diced pineapple	1 egg white
½ cup diced mango	Salt and freshly ground pepper
½ cup diced papaya	1 cup panko breadcrumbs
½ cup chopped red onions	½ cup macadamia nuts
1 tsp grated lime rind	4 mahi mahi fillets (about 8 oz/250 g each),
2 tbsp lime juice	skin removed
¼ tsp hot Asian chili sauce	¼ cup vegetable oil
Salt to taste	
2 tbsp chopped fresh mint	

COMBINE pineapple, mango, papaya, onions, lime rind, lime juice and chili sauce in a bowl. Season with salt and stir in mint.

PREPARE fish by beating egg white in a shallow bowl until frothy. Season with salt and pepper.

COMBINE panko and nuts in a food processor and process until finely chopped. Transfer to a shallow dish.

SEASON fish fillets with salt and pepper. Dip fillets into egg white and then into nut mixture.

HEAT oil in a large skillet over medium heat. Add fillets and fry for about 3 minutes on each side, or until golden brown. Remove to serving plates and garnish with salsa.

{ panko }

Panko are fried Japanese breadcrumbs that give food a crisp coating. They can be found in most supermarkets, but buy trans fats-free panko if possible. For a passable substitute, brown fresh breadcrumbs in butter, or just use regular dry breadcrumbs.

Cod Poached with Asian Flavourings

SERVES 4

This Asian-inspired all-in-one dish works well with juicy cod or grouper. It is lower-fat than many Asian curry dishes because it does not contain coconut milk.

This recipe calls for coriander leaves and stems (the stems contain more flavour than the leaves). If your bok choy are tiny, use twice as many.

3 cups chicken or fish stock

1 tbsp grated gingerroot

3 fresh coriander stems

1 clove garlic, sliced

2 tbsp fish sauce or soy sauce

2 tbsp rice vinegar

1 tsp grated lemon rind

1 tsp granulated sugar

$^1/_2$ tsp hot Asian chili sauce

4 cod fillets (about 5 oz/150 g each), skin removed

Salt and freshly ground pepper

4 baby bok choy, halved

4 large shiitake mushrooms, stemmed and
    quartered

2 cups cooked rice or rice noodles

$^1/_4$ cup chopped fresh coriander

COMBINE stock, ginger, coriander stems, garlic, fish sauce, vinegar, lemon rind, sugar and chili sauce in a skillet large enough to hold fish in one layer. Bring to a boil over medium heat, reduce heat and simmer gently for 10 minutes.

SEASON fish lightly with salt and pepper. Add fish to broth. Add bok choy and mushrooms. Cover and poach fish for 10 to 12 minutes, or until fish is opaque all the way through.

PLACE a spoonful of rice in centre of individual rimmed soup plates. Place fish on top. Surround with vegetables and pour a little broth over top. Garnish with coriander.

{ poaching fish }

Poaching means cooking food in liquid that is 180 F, or just bubbling gently. It is a light, flavourful method for cooking fish, as the flavour of the liquid is imparted to the fish and it does not break up the delicate flesh. Cod, sea bass, sole or flounder all poach well.

Thai Salmon Cakes with Sesame Aioli

SERVES 4

These fish cakes can also be made very small and served as hors d'oeuvres. If snow pea greens are not available, use red leaf lettuce.

Sesame Aioli

½ cup mayonnaise

¼ cup sour cream

2 tbsp sesame oil

1 tsp minced garlic

2 tbsp lime juice

Salt and freshly ground pepper

Salmon Cakes

1 stalk lemongrass

½ cup coarsely chopped fresh coriander leaves
 and stems

1 tsp hot Asian chili sauce

2 tsp grated lime rind

1 tbsp fish sauce

1 egg yolk

1 lb (500 g) salmon, skin removed, cubed

Salt and freshly ground pepper

2 tbsp vegetable oil

4 cups snow pea greens

1 tbsp black sesame seeds

COMBINE mayonnaise, sour cream, sesame oil, garlic and lime juice in a bowl. Season with salt and pepper.

PREPARE salmon cakes by removing tender base of lemongrass stalk and discarding top. Remove any tough outer leaves. Smash lemongrass bulb with flat side of a heavy knife to release juices. Chop lemongrass and then combine in a food processor with coriander, hot chili sauce and lime rind. Process until finely chopped.

ADD fish sauce, egg yolk and salmon to food processor. Season with salt and pepper. Pulse until mixture is well combined but still retains some texture. Form mixture into 4 cakes.

HEAT oil in a large non-stick skillet over medium heat. Fry fish cakes for 2 minutes per side, or until cakes are crisp and browned outside and slightly rare and juicy in middle. Serve fish cakes on a bed of snow pea greens. Add a dollop of aioli and sprinkle with sesame seeds.

CHILI SAUCES • Hot Asian chili sauce is very hot, and it adds a real zing to dishes. I like sambal oelek, a slightly chunky, fresh-tasting mixture containing only chilies with a little added vinegar. Hot Thai chili sauce, also called sriracha, is much smoother and a little mellower as it contains vinegar, salt, sugar and sometimes garlic. Sweet Thai chili sauce is much sweeter and is used on its own as a marinade or as a dip with spring rolls.

CORIANDER • A fragrant herb known as cilantro in Spanish-speaking countries. It is used to flavour Asian and Mexican dishes. If you have a real aversion to it, substitute fresh mint or basil.

FISH SAUCE • Fish sauce is made from fermented small fish and salt. The liquid that is obtained after fermentation is boiled down to produce a clear, salty liquid that mellows as it cooks. It is indispensable in Thai cooking.

LEMONGRASS • Lemongrass is a fragrant, fibrous lemon flavoured stalk used to flavour Asian soups and Thai curries. It is often cooked in large pieces and strained out before serving. To use it in a sauce or marinade, cut off the top and the bottom 2 inches and remove a few outer leaves. Pound the stalk to a pulp before mixing with other herbs and spices.

RICE VINEGAR • Most commonly associated with Asian cooking, it adds a nice touch to many Western dishes, too. Made from fermented rice, it is less acidic than regular vinegars and has a sweeter, milder taste. Regular Japanese rice vinegar is a subtle, golden vinegar with very low acidity. The seasoned version (sometimes called sushi vinegar) is pre-seasoned with sugar and salt and is often used to flavour sushi rice. If you don't have rice vinegar, dilute white wine vinegar or cider vinegar with a little water.

SESAME OIL • An aromatic oil made from toasted sesame seeds. It is usually used to add flavour to a dish. I prefer the flavourful Japanese sesame oil, because its quality never varies. It is too strong to cook with, but a drop added to some vegetable oil will add a good sesame flavour to stir-fries.

Salmon with Red Chili Sauce

SERVES 4

This outstanding, mildly flavoured sauce can also be used with pork or seafood. It keeps for up to two weeks, refrigerated.

Serve the salmon with warm flour tortillas or corn bread. It is also excellent cold.

½ cup chopped onions	**Salmon**
1 tbsp chopped garlic	4 salmon fillets (about 6 oz/175 g each), skin on
3 plum tomatoes, chopped	½ tsp ancho chili powder
2 tsp honey	Salt
2 tbsp ancho chili powder	2 tbsp chopped fresh coriander
1 tsp dried oregano	
1 tsp ground cumin	
3 tbsp lime juice	
Salt and freshly ground pepper	

PREHEAT oven to 350 F.

COMBINE onions, garlic, tomatoes, honey, chili powder, oregano and cumin in a small pot over medium heat. Bring to a boil, reduce heat and simmer for 20 minutes, or until mixture has thickened. Blend in a food processor or with a hand blender until smooth, adding a little water if mixture is too thick.

ADD lime juice and season well with salt and pepper. Transfer sauce to a baking dish.

SEASON salmon with chili powder and salt. Place salmon on sauce. Bake, uncovered, for 16 to 18 minutes, or until salmon is firm to the touch and white juices begin to appear. Sprinkle with coriander before serving.

{ chili powder }

Chili powder is usually a mixture of chilies, cumin and other seasonings. Pure chili powder that contains only dried chilies has much more flavour. The heat will vary, depending on the kind of chilies.

New Mexican or ancho chili powder is available at Latin American stores and some gourmet food shops. The ancho chilies have a chocolaty, piquant flavour but not a lot of heat. If unavailable, use regular chili powder, or you can buy dried ancho chilies and pulverize them in a spice mill to make your own powder.

Simon's Trout with Pernod

SERVES 2

Simon Houghton is a man with a mission. Hawley House, the bed and breakfast that he operates on the north shore of Tasmania, is more than just an excellent place to eat and stay. It's also a refuge for native animals and plants and the rare ducks and fish that he stocks in the lakes on the property. The place is his family home, and he expects guests to feel like members of the family.

The vegetables he serves in his restaurant come from his large organic gardens. He buys from local fishermen and grows his own grapes to make organic wine. It's a little piece of paradise.

This is his signature dish.

1 tbsp olive oil	2 tbsp Pernod or anisette
Salt and freshly ground pepper	$\frac{1}{4}$ cup butter
$\frac{1}{4}$ cup lime juice	1 tsp crushed fennel seeds
2 whole rainbow trout, cleaned	2 tbsp chopped parsley

COMBINE oil, salt, pepper and 2 tbsp lime juice in a small bowl. Brush mixture over trout.

PREHEAT grill on high heat. Grill trout for 5 minutes per side, or until flesh is just pink next to the bone. Place trout on serving plates.

HEAT Pernod in a small pot and bring to a boil. Boil until 1 tbsp remains. Add butter, fennel seeds, remaining 2 tbsp lime juice and parsley. Return to a boil and pour sauce over fish.

Grilled Pickerel with Lemon Garlic Sauce

SERVES 4

Pickerel is a delicate, sweet-tasting fish, but you can also use white snapper or trout in this recipe. Use whole fish and have the fishmonger clean them for you. Leave the head intact and remove it before serving.

2 whole pickerel, cleaned	**Lemon Garlic Sauce**
2 tbsp olive oil	2 tsp minced garlic
Salt and freshly ground pepper	2 tbsp lemon juice
1 bulb fennel, trimmed	1/4 cup olive oil
	1/4 cup chopped fresh mint or parsley
	Salt and freshly ground pepper

BRUSH or spray fish lightly with oil. Season fish inside and out with salt and pepper.

CUT fennel into slices 1/2 inch thick.

PREPARE sauce by whisking garlic, lemon juice, oil and mint in a bowl. Season with salt and pepper.

PREHEAT grill on high. Place fennel slices on grill and lay fish on top. Grill for 15 minutes. Turn fish and grill second side for about 10 minutes, or until flesh is opaque. Discard fennel (it will be too burnt to eat) and serve fish drizzled with sauce.

{ grilling whole fish }

Start with olive oil or vegetable oil in a spray pump, and use it to oil the fish, the grill and grill basket if using.

A grill basket is good for barbecuing whole fish (the fish is easy to turn, and it doesn't stick to the barbecue), but my current favourite method for grilling whole fish was shown to me by Michael Potters, chef/owner of Harvest Restaurant in Picton, Prince Edward County, Ontario. He lays fennel slices on the grill and places the fish on top. The fennel flavours the fish and prevents it from sticking to the grill.

Cook whole fish until the eye turns white and the flesh near the bone is slightly pink. The fish will keep cooking after it has been removed from the grill. Remove the top skin before serving if you wish.

Pepper Tuna

SERVES 4

The deep flavour of the peppercorns contrasts beautifully with the tuna in this fish version of pepper steak.

3 tbsp olive oil

4 tuna steaks (about 8 oz/250 g each)

2 tbsp cracked peppercorns

Salt

1/2 cup red wine

1 tbsp balsamic vinegar

1 cup fish or chicken stock

2 tbsp whipping cream

Salt and freshly ground pepper

RUB 2 tbsp oil on tuna steaks and sprinkle both sides of tuna with peppercorns and salt.

HEAT a large non-stick skillet over high heat. Add remaining 1 tbsp oil and heat. Add tuna. Fry for 2 minutes. Turn and fry for 2 to 3 minutes longer, depending on thickness of fish. Fish should be rare, but if you prefer it more well done, cook for another 2 minutes. Transfer tuna to serving plates.

ADD wine to skillet and cook for 2 to 3 minutes, or until 2 tbsp remains. Add vinegar and stock and continue to cook for about 5 minutes, or until 1/2 cup remains.

ADD cream, bring to a boil and boil for about 2 minutes, or just until sauce begins to thicken. Season with salt and pepper. Spoon sauce around tuna.

{ cracking peppercorns }

To crack peppercorns or seeds such as coriander, allspice and cumin, place in a plastic bag and bash with the base of a pot or rolling pin until they crack open.

Spiced Mussels in White Wine

This rich dish is particularly good served with some great bread to mop up all the juices. The spicy, creamy sauce complements the sweetness of the mussels.

1 tbsp butter	1 cup white wine
½ cup finely chopped onions	2 lb (1 kg) mussels
½ tsp chopped garlic	1 cup whipping cream
1 tsp Indian curry powder	2 tbsp chopped parsley
½ tsp fennel seeds	Salt and freshly ground pepper

HEAT butter in a large pot over medium-high heat. Add onions, garlic, curry powder and fennel seeds and sauté for 1 minute. Add wine and bring to a boil.

STIR in mussels, cover and cook, shaking pot occasionally, for 3 minutes, or until mussels open. Remove mussels from pot. Discard any mussels that haven't opened.

COOK liquid in pot for about 5 minutes, or until reduced by half. Stir in cream and cook for 3 minutes, or until slightly thickened. Add parsley and season with salt and pepper. Return mussels to pot, stir everything together and serve.

{ mussels }

Fresh mussels and clams are cooked when they are still alive. When

you buy them, make sure they are tightly closed. If they are open and don't close when you tap them, it means they are dead and should be thrown out. Conversely, if the shells don't open when they are steamed, they are also dead and should be discarded.

Cultivated mussels, which are grown in long nylon stockings in bays, are cleaner and fatter than wild mussels. Remove the beards (the feathery hairs sprouting from the shell) before cooking.

Mussels can be stored for up to three days in the coldest part of the refrigerator.

Fresh and Spicy Scallop Curry

SERVES 2 TO 3

The pungent taste of vinegar balances this marvellous dish nicely. Serve the curry over rice.

1 tsp ground cumin	1 tbsp finely chopped garlic
1 tsp ground turmeric	2 tbsp finely chopped fresh coriander
2 tsp Indian curry paste	1 cup chopped canned tomatoes
3 tbsp rice or wine vinegar	1 cup juice from canned tomatoes
2 tbsp vegetable oil	1 lb (500 g) large scallops
2 cups chopped onions	Salt and freshly ground pepper
1 tbsp finely chopped gingerroot	

COMBINE cumin, turmeric, curry paste and 2 tbsp vinegar in a small bowl. Reserve.

HEAT oil in a large skillet over low heat. Add onions and cook, stirring occasionally, for 10 minutes, or until soft. Add ginger and garlic and continue to cook, stirring, for 5 minutes, or until soft and slightly coloured.

ADD coriander and curry paste mixture. Cook, stirring, for 1 minute. Raise heat to medium, stir in tomatoes and juice and bring to a boil. Reduce heat and simmer for 5 minutes.

ADD scallops, cover and cook for 5 minutes, or until scallops are opaque.

POUR in remaining vinegar and season with salt and pepper.

{ curry seasonings }

I generally prefer to use Indian curry paste rather than curry powder, because the spices have been blended with oil and precooked to remove the raw taste. Curry pastes are sold in tins or jars in Asian grocery stores and some supermarkets and are excellent in homemade Indian curries. They can be mild, medium or hot. Choose the one best suited to your palate (I use medium).

Thai curry pastes can be red, green or yellow. Red curry paste is made with red chilies. Green curry paste is made with green chilies, lemongrass, kaffir lime leaves and other herbs and spices; it is the hottest of the three. Yellow curry paste is the mildest; it contains turmeric (which gives it its bright yellow colour) and is similar to Indian curry paste in flavour.

Seafood Boil

SERVES 6

Seafood and beer make a great combination. Place everything on the table in a large serving bowl and let people help themselves. It's messy but great fun. Serve with coleslaw and potato salad. You can also add kielbasa to this for extra flavour and texture.

2 ½ cups beer
1 cup water
8 whole garlic cloves, peeled
2 bay leaves
6 sprigs parsley
6 whole peppercorns
1 tbsp chili powder
1 tbsp lemon juice
Salt
1 lb (500 g) clams
1 lb (500 g) mussels
1 lb (500 g) large shrimp, peeled
1 lb (500 g) scallops

Lemon Butter
1 cup butter, melted
2 tbsp lemon juice
2 tsp minced garlic
2 tbsp chopped chives

COMBINE beer, water, whole garlic, bay leaves, parsley, peppercorns, chili powder, lemon juice and salt in a large pot. Bring to a boil, reduce heat and simmer for 15 minutes to combine flavours.

INCREASE heat to high, add clams and cook, uncovered, for 3 minutes. Add mussels and cook for 2 minutes. Remove shellfish to a large serving bowl as they open. Discard any clams or mussels that haven't opened.

REDUCE heat to low, add shrimp and scallops to pot and cook for 2 to 3 minutes, or until shrimp are pink and slightly curled and scallops are still opaque in centre. Remove from broth and reserve with other shellfish (discard broth).

COMBINE melted butter, lemon juice, minced garlic and chives in a bowl. Serve as a dip with shellfish.

Shrimp and Salmon with Mint and Lemon Pesto

SERVES 4

This is easy, quick cooking at its best. Use scallops instead of shrimp if desired. You could also substitute storebought basil pesto for the homemade mint pesto. Lemon balm is a lemony herb that easily grows in the garden.

Mint and Lemon Pesto
4 green onions, coarsely chopped
1 tbsp chopped garlic
½ cup fresh mint
½ cup fresh lemon balm, or ½ tsp grated
    lemon rind
1 tbsp lemon juice
¼ cup olive oil

Seafood
2 salmon fillets (about 8 oz/250 g each), skin on
8 oz (250 g) large shrimp, peeled
1 tbsp olive oil

COMBINE green onions, garlic, mint, lemon balm, lemon juice and oil in a food processor or mini chop and puree until blended but still slightly chunky.

SPREAD half the pesto over salmon flesh; toss shrimp with remaining pesto.

HEAT a large skillet over medium-high heat. Add oil. When oil is hot, add salmon skin side down. Cook for 2 minutes.

REDUCE heat to medium-low, add shrimp, cover skillet and cook for 5 to 8 minutes, or until salmon is just pink in centre and shrimp are pink and curled. Cut salmon in half and serve topped with shrimp.

{ salmon }

Salmon has become a controversial fish. There is concern that some farm-raised salmon may be full of contaminants and potentially harmful to your health if you eat large quantities. Cautious people look for organic farmed salmon, which is a growing market. Wild salmon is your best bet, but it is only available fresh from about June until October.

{ cooking salmon fillets }

When you are cooking salmon fillets that are not of an even thickness, tuck the thin end pieces underneath, so the salmon will cook more evenly.

Shrimp with Lemongrass, Chili and Basil

SERVES 4

A sweet tangle of onions and shrimp with spicy undertones. Use large shrimp to protect against overcooking. The heat in this dish is personal preference, but I find that too much chili sauce masks the delicate taste of the lemongrass.

2 stalks lemongrass	1 lb (500 g) shrimp, peeled
1 tbsp finely chopped garlic	Salt and freshly ground pepper
¼ cup fish sauce	2 red onions, thinly sliced
1 to 2 tsp hot Asian chili sauce, or 1 green chili, chopped	1 tbsp granulated sugar
	1 tbsp lime juice
2 tbsp vegetable oil	½ cup shredded fresh basil

DISCARD outer leaves of lemongrass. Cut off stalks just above bulbs. Discard stalks and chop bulbs finely. You should have about 2 tbsp.

COMBINE lemongrass, 1½ tsp garlic, 2 tbsp fish sauce, chili sauce and 1 tbsp oil in a large bowl. Stir in shrimp, season with salt and pepper and marinate for 30 minutes.

HEAT a wok or large skillet over medium-high heat. Add remaining 1 tbsp oil and heat. Add onions and remaining 1½ tsp garlic and stir-fry for 6 minutes, or until onions turn golden.

ADD shrimp and marinade, remaining 2 tbsp fish sauce and sugar. Stir-fry for 2 minutes, or until shrimp is just cooked.

ADD lime juice and basil. Continue to cook for about 1 minute, or until basil wilts. Serve at once.

{ shrimp }

Most shrimp that we buy (unless you live on the east or west coast) are frozen when caught. They are defrosted before you buy them, so should not be refrozen. Black tiger shrimp, which are mostly farmed, have great texture, but I prefer American whites, which have more flavour.

To peel shrimp, pull off the legs. Grasp the shell between your thumb and forefinger and pull it off.

I do not normally devein shrimp, but if you feel you must, just cut along the outer curve of the body with a sharp knife, and the vein will come away.

Cassoulet of Mussels and Clams

SERVES 4 AS A SIDE DISH

This is my take on a dish served at the Creel Restaurant in Orkney. Located in the tiny village of St. Margaret's Hope, it is run by a husband-and-wife team who serve some of the best food in Scotland. Serve it on its own or with any plainly grilled or baked white fish.

½ cup white wine	1 tbsp chopped garlic
18 clams	1 19-oz (540 mL) can Romano beans, rinsed and drained
18 mussels	
3 tbsp olive oil	2 tbsp chopped parsley
½ cup chopped chorizo	Salt and freshly ground pepper
½ cup chopped shallots	¼ cup fresh breadcrumbs

PLACE wine in a large pot and bring to a boil over medium-high heat. Add clams, cover and cook for 5 minutes. Add mussels, cover and cook for about 3 minutes, or until clams and mussels open. Strain liquid into a bowl and reserve. Remove clams and mussels from shells and reserve.

HEAT 2 tbsp oil in a large skillet over medium heat. Add chorizo and shallots and sauté for 3 minutes, or until soft.

ADD garlic and sauté for 1 minute. Add beans and sauté for 2 minutes, or until heated through. Add reserved cooking liquid and simmer for about 10 minutes, or until liquid has reduced to a sauce and flavours meld.

STIR in cooked clams, mussels and parsley. Season with salt and pepper. Remove from heat.

HEAT remaining 1 tbsp oil in a small skillet over medium heat. Add breadcrumbs and cook, stirring, for 3 minutes, or until golden. Serve cassoulet sprinkled with breadcrumbs.

{ chorizo }

Chorizo is a mild or spicy Spanish or Portuguese sausage that comes fresh or smoked. I like to use the smoked version in traditional Spanish dishes. Substitute any other spicy smoked sausage, or use kielbasa and add ½ tsp chili flakes.

{ poultry }

Roast Chicken

SERVES 4

I learned how to roast a chicken the first day I attended the Cordon Bleu, and this method has been my standby ever since.

This recipe can easily be adapted according to your tastes. Sprinkle the chicken with a tablespoon of chopped fresh herbs; place lemon or orange slices in the cavity; brush the skin with curry paste mixed with a little vegetable oil; or brush with a mixture of soy sauce, grated ginger and sesame oil.

For a crisp skin, it is important to use kosher salt. You can also put quartered onions and whole cloves of garlic under the chicken while it is roasting to add flavour to the sauce.

1 chicken (about 4 lb/2 kg)	1 tbsp all-purpose flour
2 tbsp butter, at room temperature	1 ½ cups chicken stock
2 tsp kosher salt	1 tsp balsamic vinegar
Freshly ground pepper	

PREHEAT oven to 400 F.

TWIST wing tips and tuck under wingbones. Rub butter over chicken skin and pop a little inside cavity. Season with salt and pepper. Tie legs together with string to keep shape compact.

PLACE chicken breast side up on a rack in a roasting pan. Roast for 1 hour and 15 minutes, or until juices run clear. Let chicken rest on a carving board for 10 minutes.

DISCARD all but 2 tbsp fat from roasting pan. Heat pan over medium heat. Add flour and cook, stirring, for 1 minute, or until flour turns golden brown.

POUR in stock and bring to a boil, scraping up bits from bottom of roasting pan. Add vinegar and any accumulated juices from carving board and simmer for 2 minutes. Season with salt and pepper.

CARVE chicken and serve drizzled with sauce.

The best chicken is free range and organic. It has so much flavour that not

much needs to be done to make it mouth-watering. If this is not an option, then free-range
naturally raised chickens (raised without antibiotics but not necessarily fed with organic
feed) are also excellent.

At the supermarket level, look for an air-chilled chicken that is chilled naturally, not in
water. It has a more even yellow colour, and the meat looks quite glossy. If you can, avoid
those white, battery-raised supermarket chickens and turkeys; they just don't deliver the taste
and texture. Try to buy fresh whenever possible, as freezing alters the texture of poultry.

My roasting method differs from many others, because I roast on high

heat, which results in a crisper skin and juicier bird.

To roast a turkey, chicken or capon, preheat the oven to 400 F. Roast for 15 minutes per
pound (500 g) plus 15 extra minutes. If the poultry is stuffed, count the stuffing as an additional pound.

When roasting turkey, remember that any bird weighing more than 10 lb (5 kg) cooks
from the inside as well as the outside and requires less cooking time. Therefore, after 10 lb
(5 kg), reduce the cooking time to 7 minutes per pound (500 g). For example, a 14-lb (7 kg)
turkey will cook for 150 minutes for the first 10 lb (5 kg) and 28 minutes for the last 4 lb
(2 kg), giving a total cooking time of about 3 hours.

As far as basting is concerned, after much experimenting, I've found that basting an
oven-roasted chicken seldom alters the taste or texture. The only time I baste now is when
the skin seems dry.

TRUSSING • Trussing poultry is not absolutely necessary, but it does help the bird
keep its shape and helps protect the breast meat from becoming overcooked.

Cut a piece of string four times the length of the bird. Place the string under the back
and wing section, bringing the ends up to breast level. Draw both ends of string across the
body and hook around the tips of the drumsticks. Pull the string up over the legs, cross over
and bring both ends around the tail. Tie string in a bow around the legs for easier removal
after roasting. If the bird is stuffed, use a metal skewer to close the cavity.

Cabernet Chicken

SERVES 4

This method of pot-roasting chicken produces a juicy, golden bird with a marvellous sauce. If your grapes have seeds, slice them in half and flick out the seeds with the point of a knife. You can use red or green grapes in this dish (the taste and colour of the sauce will depend on which grapes you use).

1 chicken (about 3 lb/1.5 kg)
Salt and freshly ground pepper
1 tbsp butter
1 cup sliced leeks
1/2 cup chopped carrots
1/4 cup chopped celery
1 tbsp chopped fresh tarragon or oregano,
    or 1 tsp dried

1 cup red wine
1/2 cup seedless red grapes, halved

Garnish
1/2 cup whole seedless red grapes
Sprigs of fresh chervil or tarragon

PREHEAT oven to 400 F.

SEASON chicken with salt and pepper. Truss chicken to help it keep its shape.

HEAT butter in a casserole over medium heat. Brown chicken breast side down until golden, about 3 minutes. Continue to brown chicken on all sides for about 3 minutes per side. Remove chicken from casserole and drain off all but 1 tbsp fat.

ADD leeks, carrots and celery to casserole and sauté for 2 minutes, or until softened. Add tarragon and wine. Bring to a boil and cook for about 5 minutes, or until reduced by half. Stir in grape halves and return chicken to pan breast side up.

BAKE chicken, covered, basting occasionally, for 55 minutes, or until juices run clear. Remove chicken from casserole to a carving board and cover with a tea towel to keep warm. Let rest for 10 minutes.

SKIM fat from liquid in casserole. Strain sauce into a skillet, pressing down on solids (discard solids). Add whole grapes to sauce, bring to a boil and simmer for 1 minute, or until flavours are combined. Taste and adjust seasonings if necessary. Carve chicken and serve with sauce. Garnish with chervil.

Chicken Adobo

SERVES 4

Adobo is the national dish of the Philippines, made with chicken, pork or fish. This is an excellent make-ahead dish, as the vinegar keeps the chicken moist, and in fact the flavour is best if the dish is made a day ahead. Serve it with rice.

1 chicken (about 3 lb/1.5 kg), cut in 8 pieces	1/2 tsp hot Asian chili sauce
1/4 cup finely chopped garlic	2 bay leaves
Salt	3/4 cup water
2 tsp cracked peppercorns	2 tbsp olive oil
1/2 cup rice vinegar	1 onion, sliced
1/4 cup soy sauce	2 cups baby spinach

COMBINE chicken, garlic, salt, peppercorns, vinegar, soy sauce, chili sauce and bay leaves in a casserole or pot. Marinate for 30 minutes.

ADD water to casserole, arranging chicken so it is mostly submerged in cooking liquid, and bring to a boil. Reduce heat and simmer, uncovered, until chicken is just cooked, about 25 minutes. Remove chicken to a plate and pat dry with a paper towel. Strain cooking liquid into a bowl and skim off any fat.

HEAT oil in a large non-stick skillet over medium heat. Add chicken and brown on both sides for about 5 minutes in total. Transfer chicken back to casserole.

ADD onions to skillet and sauté until tender, about 3 minutes. Transfer onions to casserole.

ADD reserved cooking liquid to skillet, bring to a boil and boil for 1 minute, scraping bottom of pan to dissolve any brown bits. Stir in spinach.

POUR contents of skillet over chicken and onions. Cool. Refrigerate until needed. Reheat on top of stove for 10 to 15 minutes, or until everything is hot.

Very Crisp Fried Chicken with Walnut Sauce

SERVES 2 TO 3

This recipe makes a gorgeous, succulent chicken. Weighting the bird makes it cook evenly and crisply. Have the butcher butterfly and remove the breast and backbone for you if possible.

Traditionally this dish is cooked under a brick, but a weighted plate works fine. If you have two large skillets, you can double the recipe and cook two chickens at the same time. (This recipe will serve up to four if the meal includes a first course and dessert.)

Garnish this with radishes and thinly sliced red onions. You can serve it with plain garlic butter instead of the walnut sauce, if preferred. It is perfect cold, too.

1 chicken (about 3 lb/1.5 kg)	**Garlic Walnut Sauce**
Salt and freshly ground pepper	1/2 cup walnuts, toasted and chopped
Pinch paprika	2 tsp chopped garlic
1 tbsp vegetable oil	1/4 cup chopped fresh coriander
1 tbsp butter	1/4 tsp ground coriander
	Pinch cayenne
	1 tbsp olive oil
	1/4 cup chicken stock
	1 tbsp lemon juice
	Salt and freshly ground pepper

CUT chicken along both sides of backbone and remove backbone. Pull out breastbone. Cut off wing tips.

PLACE chicken skin side up on a board and cover with wax paper. With a mallet or bottom of a pot, flatten chicken until it is an even thickness. Rub skin with salt, pepper and paprika. Tuck legs into breasts to make a tidy bird that will cook evenly.

HEAT oil and butter in a large skillet over medium heat. Add chicken skin side down and place a plate or pan that fits inside skillet over chicken. Place heavy cans or other weights on plate. Reduce heat to medium-low and cook for 20 minutes. Carefully pour off fat, turn chicken, return plate and weights and cook skin side up for 10 to 15 minutes, or until cooked through and juices run clear.

PREPARE sauce while chicken is cooking. Combine walnuts, garlic, fresh and ground coriander, cayenne, oil, stock and lemon juice in a food processor or by hand. Mixture should have some texture. Season with salt and pepper.

CUT chicken into serving pieces and serve with sauce.

Indian Spiced Chicken

SERVES 4

Serve with chutney, sliced red onions and tomatoes sprinkled with lemon juice and fresh coriander.

2 tbsp chopped gingerroot	1 tbsp lemon juice
2 tbsp chopped garlic	1 tbsp Indian curry paste
1 tsp garam masala	3 tbsp vegetable oil
1 tsp chopped jalapeño	4 boneless chicken breasts, skin on
¼ cup chopped fresh mint	Salt and freshly ground pepper

PREHEAT oven to 425 F.

COMBINE ginger, garlic, garam masala, jalapeño, mint, lemon juice, curry paste and oil in a food processor or by hand. Brush all over chicken and skin, and inside where there is a natural opening between filet and breast. Season with salt and pepper.

ARRANGE chicken breasts skin side up in a baking dish in a single layer. Bake for 20 to 25 minutes, or until juices run clear and skin is crisp. Remove from oven and let rest for 5 minutes before cutting into ½-inch slices.

{ garam masala }

Garam ("hot spices") masala is a fragrant spice blend that has layers of flavour as opposed to just being hot. It can be used like a curry powder but it is often added at the end of cooking.

In India, the mix of spices varies from city to city and from kitchen to kitchen. You can buy garam masala, but making your own will add a fresh taste to everything you use it in.

Place 2 tbsp cardamom seeds, two 3-inch cinnamon sticks, 1 tbsp whole cloves, 3 tbsp whole black peppercorns, ½ cup cumin seeds and ½ cup coriander seeds in a dry skillet over medium heat. Cook, stirring frequently, for 1 to 2 minutes, or until spices darken slightly and smell fragrant. Remove from heat immediately. Grind in a coffee grinder or spice grinder until powdery. Cool and store in an airtight jar for up to 6 months.

Makes about 1¼ cups.

Steamed Chicken Breasts with Baby Bok Choy and Shiitake Mushrooms

SERVES 4

Steaming brings out the natural flavours of food, and it is an underrated and low-fat cooking technique. Oven-steaming (as in this recipe), rather than steaming on the stove over water, allows you to cook more food at one time.

Serve this with rice.

1 tsp grated lime rind	4 boneless, skinless chicken breasts
2 tbsp chopped fresh mint	Salt and freshly ground pepper
2 tbsp chopped fresh basil	4 baby bok choy, halved if large
2 tsp soy sauce	1 small red pepper, seeded and diced
2 tbsp rice vinegar	6 shiitake mushrooms, stemmed and thinly sliced
1 tsp granulated sugar	½ cup chicken stock
1 tbsp vegetable oil	1 tbsp chopped parsley

COMBINE lime rind, mint, basil, soy sauce, vinegar, sugar and oil in a large bowl. Add chicken and toss with marinade. Marinate for 2 to 12 hours, refrigerated.

PREHEAT oven to 325 F.

ARRANGE chicken, along with any marinade, in a single layer in a large baking dish. Season with salt and pepper. Scatter bok choy, red pepper and mushrooms around chicken. Pour stock over chicken. Cover with foil.

BAKE for 30 to 35 minutes, or until chicken and vegetables are tender and chicken juices run clear. Serve garnished with parsley.

Mushroom-stuffed Chicken with Vegetables

SERVES 4

An all-in-one-dish main course. The chicken has much more flavour if the skin is left on, and it adds texture to the dish.

2 tbsp butter	4 boneless chicken breasts, skin on
1 tsp chopped garlic	2 tbsp olive oil
2 cups finely chopped mixed mushrooms	2 Asian eggplants or zucchini, sliced in rounds
1 tsp chopped fresh thyme, or 1/4 tsp dried	2 leeks, white and light-green parts only, sliced
2 tbsp chopped fresh mint	16 cherry tomatoes, halved
2 tbsp fresh breadcrumbs	1/4 cup white wine
1/4 cup whipping cream	1/2 cup chicken stock
Salt and freshly ground pepper	1/4 cup chopped chives

PREHEAT oven to 400 F.

HEAT butter in a large skillet over medium heat. Add garlic and sauté for 1 minute. Add mushrooms and thyme and sauté for about 2 minutes, or until mushrooms release their juices. Stir in mint, breadcrumbs and cream and cook for about 1 minute, or until mixture thickens. Season with salt and pepper. Cool.

SLIP fingers under skin of chicken to create a pocket. Make sure one edge is still attached to breast. Stuff mushroom mixture under chicken skin. Pat down to flatten stuffing slightly. Season skin with salt and pepper.

HEAT oil in a large ovenproof skillet over medium heat. Brown chicken, skin side down, for 2 minutes. Cook second side for 1 minute, or until browned. Remove chicken from skillet and reserve.

ADD eggplants to skillet and sauté for 2 minutes, or until slightly softened. Add leeks and tomatoes and cook for 2 minutes. Add wine and bring to a boil.

PLACE chicken breasts on vegetables and bake, uncovered, for 10 minutes. Add stock and bake for 10 to 15 minutes longer, or until chicken juices run clear. Remove breasts and keep warm.

BOIL down sauce with vegetables on top of stove for 1 to 2 minutes, or until slightly thickened. Serve with chicken. Garnish with chives.

The Ultimate Chicken Sandwich

SERVES 6

This is not your usual chicken sandwich. It is really a chicken meatloaf with a bread crust. This dish is based on an idea from my late mother, Pearl Geneen. It is one of my most requested recipes and my son-in-law Micah's favourite. It is truly wonderful.

It is best to chop your own chicken thighs because they are juicier than chicken breasts (boned and skinned chicken thighs are available at the supermarket). Use an inexpensive white bread for rolling, because good bread won't flatten out properly. You can also make this with ground chicken or turkey.

2 lb (500 g) boneless, skinless chicken thighs	½ cup dry breadcrumbs
2 eggs, beaten	1 bunch watercress or arugula, trimmed and
1 cup finely chopped onions	roughly chopped
2 tsp finely chopped garlic	Salt and freshly ground pepper
1 tbsp finely chopped fresh rosemary or tarragon,	6 slices white sandwich bread, crusts removed
or 1 tsp dried	2 tbsp vegetable oil

PREHEAT oven to 375 F.

CHOP chicken into small chunks in a food processor or by hand, leaving some texture in chicken.

COMBINE chicken, eggs, onions, garlic, rosemary, breadcrumbs and watercress in a bowl. Season with salt and pepper. Fry a bit to taste for seasoning.

ROLL out bread slices very thinly. Brush both sides of bread with oil. Place 3 slices slightly overlapping on an oiled baking sheet. Pile chicken mixture on top and shape to cover bread. Top with remaining bread slices and press down lightly.

BAKE for 30 to 40 minutes, or until white juices start to appear. Bread should be crisp and golden on both sides. Cut into serving pieces. Serve hot or cold.

{ ground chicken }

Ground chicken ranges from extra-lean to about 20 percent fat. The fat makes it juicy—better for meatloaf and chicken burgers. You can sometimes find ground dark-meat chicken in the kosher sections of supermarkets, as well as ground dark-meat turkey, which can be used as a substitute for chicken.

Grilled Chicken with Aigre-douce Sauce

SERVES 4

Aigre-douce is French for sweet and sour, but this sauce has a little more sophistication than the thick, glutinous Asian sauces. I use pomegranate juice as the base, and it results in a beautiful ruby-red sauce. Serve this with green vegetables and steamed rice.

Chicken
1 tsp chopped garlic
1/2 tsp grated lime rind
2 tbsp Dijon mustard
2 tbsp olive oil
2 tbsp chopped fresh coriander
4 boneless, skinless chicken breasts
Salt and freshly ground pepper

Aigre-douce Sauce
1/4 cup chopped shallots
2 cups pomegranate juice
2 tbsp brown sugar
1/2 cup cider vinegar

COMBINE garlic, lime rind, mustard, oil and coriander in a small bowl. Rub on chicken and marinate for 30 minutes. Season chicken with salt and pepper.

COMBINE shallots, pomegranate juice, sugar and vinegar in a pot. Bring to a boil. Reduce heat and simmer for about 8 minutes, or until slightly syrupy.

PREHEAT grill on high and grill chicken for 5 to 7 minutes per side, or until juices run clear. Serve chicken with sauce.

{ pomegranates }

Aside from being very tasty, pomegranates are a great health food, containing three times more antioxidants than green tea or red wine. Their flavour is sweet but with a tangy touch. They come to the market ripe and keep for 3 months, refrigerated, if they are stored in a plastic bag. The juice flavours sauces and thickens nicely when reduced, and the seeds add colour, texture and flavour to salads, main courses and desserts. Hollowed-out pome-granates also make exceptional candle holders to decorate the table for holiday entertaining.

To peel a pomegranate, cut the crown off the fruit. Score the skin in quarters and bend back each quarter. Scoop the seeds into a bowl. One pomegranate yields about 3/4 cup seeds and 1/2 cup juice. The seeds can be frozen for later use.

To obtain the juice, squeeze as much out of the pomegranate as you can, then add the seeds to a blender and blend until pulpy. Press through a sieve.

Cinnamon Gardens Chicken Curry

SERVES 8

An excellent fragrant curry to eat with Indian bread or rice. Use a curry paste that suits your taste—mild, medium or hot.

2 tbsp vegetable oil

2 cups finely chopped onions

1 tbsp finely chopped gingerroot

1 tbsp finely chopped garlic

2 tbsp Indian curry paste

1 tsp ground cinnamon

1 tsp ground coriander

1 tsp ground cumin

2 lb (1 kg) boneless, skinless chicken breasts,
    cut in 2-inch pieces

Salt and freshly ground pepper

1 cup coconut milk

2 cups chopped canned tomatoes

2 cups baby spinach

1 cup raisins

1 tbsp lemon juice

2 tbsp chopped fresh coriander

HEAT oil in a large wok or skillet over medium-low heat. Add onions and cook slowly for about 10 minutes, or until softened and browned on edges. Add ginger and garlic. Cook for 5 minutes longer.

STIR in curry paste, cinnamon, coriander and cumin and cook for about 1 minute, or until fragrant.

RAISE heat to medium-high, add chicken and sauté for about 4 minutes, or until coated with spices and slightly browned. Season with salt and pepper and remove chicken to a bowl.

ADD coconut milk and tomatoes to wok and stir in, scraping up any bits on bottom of pan. Bring to a boil. Reduce heat and simmer for 5 minutes, or until thickened.

RETURN chicken to pan and simmer, uncovered, for 4 to 5 minutes, or until chicken is almost cooked through. Add spinach and raisins and cook for 5 minutes longer. Stir in lemon juice. Taste for seasoning, adding salt or lemon juice as needed. Sprinkle with coriander.

Crispy Chicken Legs with Savoury Stuffing

SERVES 4

A mouth-watering way to prepare chicken legs. Have your butcher remove the top bone that attaches the leg to the chicken and the thigh bone too. Use a hot or sweet Italian sausage.

2 tsp olive oil

½ cup chopped onions

1 tsp chopped garlic

2 Italian sausages, skin removed

1 cup coarsely chopped watercress

2 tbsp chopped parsley

2 tsp grated lemon rind

Salt and freshly ground pepper

4 large chicken legs, thigh bones removed

1 tbsp balsamic vinegar

¼ cup Port

½ cup chicken stock

PREHEAT oven to 400 F.

HEAT oil in a skillet over medium heat. Add onions and sauté for 3 minutes, or until softened. Add garlic and cook for 1 minute longer.

SCRAPE onion mixture into a bowl and crumble in sausage meat. Stir in watercress, parsley and lemon rind. Season with salt and pepper.

STUFF sausage mixture into chicken leg in cavity left by thigh bone. Skewer ends together. (Bake any remaining stuffing separately.) Season chicken with salt and pepper.

PLACE chicken on a rack in a roasting pan and bake for 35 to 40 minutes, or until juices run clear. Remove legs and keep warm.

SKIM fat from pan juices and place roasting pan on stove over medium heat. Add vinegar, Port and stock. Bring to a boil and cook for 2 minutes, or until sauce has reduced and thickened slightly. Season with salt and pepper. Serve sauce over chicken.

Tangy Chicken Thighs with Figs

SERVES 4

To my taste, chicken thighs are the best part of the bird. They are tasty and just fatty enough to stay juicy. This dish has a fragrant sauce with a Moroccan feel to it. Serve it with couscous.

2 tbsp olive oil	$\frac{1}{2}$ tsp ground cinnamon
2 lb (1 kg) chicken thighs, with bone and skin	$\frac{1}{2}$ tsp ground turmeric
Salt and freshly ground pepper	Pinch cayenne
1 tsp paprika	2 cups chicken stock
1 red onion, thinly sliced	8 whole dried figs
1 tsp ground coriander	2 tbsp chopped fresh mint or parsley
1 tsp ground ginger	

PREHEAT oven to 400 F.

HEAT oil in a large ovenproof skillet over medium-high heat. Season chicken thighs with salt, pepper and paprika. Fry chicken skin side down for 2 to 3 minutes, or until skin is golden. Turn and fry second side for 1 minute. Remove chicken from skillet.

DISCARD all but 1 tbsp fat from skillet. Add onions and sauté for 2 minutes, or until softened. Reduce heat to medium-low and cook for 6 to 8 minutes, or until onions are very soft.

STIR in coriander, ginger, cinnamon, turmeric and cayenne and cook for 1 minute, or until spices are fragrant.

ADD stock and bring to a boil, scraping up any spices and browned bits from bottom of pan. Boil for 5 minutes, or until stock has reduced by half.

STIR in figs. Return thighs to skillet and place in oven. Bake for 15 to 20 minutes, or until thighs are cooked through. Sprinkle with mint.

Asian Chicken with Sticky Rice

SERVES 4

This is one of my absolute favourite dishes. I love the texture of Chinese sticky rice, but you could substitute sushi rice if you wish. Serve with spicy citrus sauce.

1 cup sticky rice	Salt and freshly ground pepper
1/4 cup soy sauce	1 cup chopped onions
2 tbsp seasoned rice vinegar	1 cup diced, stemmed shiitake mushrooms
2 tsp finely chopped gingerroot	1 cup shelled edamame, defrosted
1 tsp hot Asian chili sauce	1 cup water
4 boneless, skinless chicken breasts	2 tbsp chopped fresh mint
2 tbsp vegetable oil	

RINSE rice, then soak in water for 15 minutes. Drain.

COMBINE soy sauce, vinegar, ginger and chili sauce in a small bowl. Brush half the marinade over chicken breasts.

HEAT a large skillet over medium-high heat. Add oil and heat.

SEASON chicken with salt and pepper and add to skillet. Sear for about 2 minutes per side, or until browned. Remove chicken from skillet and reserve.

ADD onions and mushrooms to skillet. Sauté until softened, about 2 minutes. Stir in rice, edamame, reserved marinade and water. Place chicken breasts on top and bring to a boil.

COVER, reduce heat to low and simmer for 10 to 15 minutes, or until chicken is cooked and rice is tender. Sprinkle with mint.

{ spicy citrus sauce }

This sauce makes a good dip for spring rolls and fresh vegetable rolls.

Combine 1 tsp grated gingerroot, 1 tsp hot Asian chili sauce, 1 tbsp brown sugar, 1 tbsp fish sauce, 2 tbsp lemon juice, 2 tbsp lime juice, 1/4 cup water and 2 tbsp chopped fresh mint in a bowl. Let sit for 1 hour before serving.

Makes about 1/2 cup.

Duck Breasts with Blood Orange Sauce

SERVES 4

Duck is my favourite poultry—the combination of crisp skin and juicy meat is unbeatable. Slowly cooking the duck breasts skin side down releases the fat and crisps the skin. Finish the cooking with a fast oven bake.

If blood oranges are unavailable (they give this dish a beautiful colour), use regular oranges.

2 duck breasts (about 1 lb/500 g each)	1 tbsp balsamic vinegar
Salt and freshly ground pepper	1/2 tsp honey
1/4 cup blood orange juice	2 cups chicken stock
1/4 cup red wine	1 tbsp butter, cold

PREHEAT oven to 450 F.

SCORE top of duck breasts in a cross-hatch pattern and season with salt and pepper. Place skin side down in a cold ovenproof skillet over medium heat. Once pan is hot, cook for 2 minutes. Reduce heat to low and cook for 15 minutes, or until fat is rendered and skin is beginning to crisp. Drain fat from skillet as it accumulates.

TURN duck breasts and place skillet in oven. Bake for 10 to 12 minutes, or until duck is medium-rare. Remove duck to a carving board and let rest for 5 minutes.

POUR any fat from skillet and return skillet to stove over medium-high heat. Stir in orange juice, wine, vinegar and honey. Bring to a boil and cook for about 2 minutes, or until reduced by half. Stir in stock and boil until sauce thickens slightly, about 5 to 8 minutes.

REDUCE heat to low and whisk in butter. Taste and adjust seasonings if necessary.

CARVE duck into 1/2-inch slices and serve with sauce.

{ duck breasts }

Duck breasts generally come from Moulard ducks, which are a cross between Muscovy and Pekin ducks. They are usually referred to as magrets and are similar to steak in texture but with a layer of fat under the skin that is slowly released during cooking.

Pekin duck breasts are smaller and less meaty but have lots of flavour. Duck breasts can be bought at some supermarkets and most butcher shops.

Turkey Breast with Prosciutto, Leeks and Cheese

SERVES 8

An easy turkey recipe for a dinner party or holiday celebration. Turkey breasts are popular because they are all white meat and contain no bones to hinder the carver.

¼ cup white wine	2 oz (60 g) thinly sliced prosciutto or
2 tbsp lemon juice	smoked ham
2 tbsp Dijon mustard	2 oz (60 g) thinly sliced Fontina cheese
2 tbsp chopped fresh rosemary, or 2 tsp dried	1 onion, sliced
1 tsp paprika	½ cup pomegranate juice
¼ cup olive oil	2 cups chicken stock
2 leeks, trimmed	Salt and freshly ground pepper
1 boneless turkey breast (about 3 to 4 lb/1.5 to 2 kg)	

COMBINE wine, lemon juice, mustard, rosemary, paprika and oil in a bowl. Reserve.

COVER leeks with cold water in a skillet and bring to a boil. Boil for 3 minutes, or until tender-crisp. Refresh leeks with cold water to stop the cooking and drain well. Slice leeks lengthwise and reserve.

LAY your hand flat on turkey breast and slice through turkey parallel to cutting board. Stop about 1 inch from edge. Open up turkey like a book and brush with some of the marinade. Lay prosciutto slices on top. Lay cheese over prosciutto and run a row of leeks down centre. Fold breast over and close opening with metal skewers or sew up with a trussing needle and string.

SPRINKLE onion slices over bottom of a roasting pan or baking dish slightly larger than turkey. Place turkey on onions and pour over remaining marinade. Marinate for 30 minutes.

PREHEAT oven to 375 F.

BAKE turkey for 1 hour 15 minutes, or until turkey juices run clear. Remove turkey to a carving board and let rest for 10 minutes.

DRAIN fat from roasting pan. Place pan on stove over medium heat. Add pomegranate juice to marinade and onions and cook, stirring, for 2 minutes, or until 2 tbsp liquid remains.

ADD stock and bring to a boil. Cook, stirring to loosen bits on bottom of pan, for 4 to 6 minutes, or until slightly thickened. Season with salt and pepper.

SLICE turkey and serve with sauce.

{ meat }

Classic Prime Rib of Beef with Pan Gravy

SERVES 8

Nothing beats the mouth-watering smell of a succulent, juicy roast in the oven. For me, roasts are symbols of celebrations and festivities. What would Thanksgiving or Christmas be without roast turkey, or Easter without roast lamb? My family (especially my stepson, Alex) are beef eaters no matter what the occasion, and we also like to celebrate birthdays with a traditional roast beef dinner.

The best roast beef is a prime rib. The first cut (from the first rib) has more of the central eye of meat and less of the fattier cap, although many people, including myself, love the rich taste of the cap.

2 tbsp Dijon mustard	1 rib roast (about 5 to 6 lb/2.5 kg to 3 kg)
2 tbsp soy sauce	Salt and freshly ground pepper
1 tbsp finely chopped garlic	2 tbsp all-purpose flour
1 tbsp chopped fresh rosemary or thyme,	¼ cup red wine
or 1 tsp dried	1½ cups beef stock
2 tbsp olive oil	1 tsp tomato paste

PREHEAT oven to 450 F, then turn on broiler.

COMBINE mustard, soy sauce, garlic, rosemary and oil in a small bowl. Brush over roast. Place meat fat side up on a rack in a roasting pan. Season with a little salt (Dijon mustard already has salt in it) and lots of pepper.

PLACE roast about 3 inches from broiler and broil for 5 minutes to help give meat a crispy fat layer. Turn off broiler.

ROAST beef at 450 F for 30 minutes. Reduce heat to 350 F and continue to roast for 1 hour to 1 hour 15 minutes for rare. Remove roast from pan and let sit for 10 minutes.

DRAIN fat and any meat juices into a measuring cup (the fat will rise to the top). Remove 2 tbsp fat and return to roasting pan. Heat on stove over medium heat. Add flour and cook, stirring, until flour is browned, about 1 minute.

ADD wine, stock and any pan juices. Scrape up any bits from bottom of roasting pan and bring to a boil, stirring. Add tomato paste. Simmer for 2 minutes. Taste and adjust seasonings if necessary. Carve beef and serve with pan gravy on the side.

I believe the best results are obtained with high-heat roasting. Although meat shrinks more when it is cooked this way, its flavour, texture and juiciness are unsurpassed. Tender cuts of beef such as sirloin, prime rib, ribeye and filet, lamb legs and veal tenderloins should all be cooked using this method.

Low heat is suitable if you are roasting pork or less tender cuts of beef, but it will rob flavour from the more tender cuts. The low-heat method dates back to the time when meat and poultry were tougher, and the lower heat was gentle on the fibres. Today, however, animals are bred to be more tender, and they need a different approach in the oven.

BASIC ROASTING TIPS

- Always roast meat on a rack placed in a roasting pan. This allows the heat to circulate, browning the underside of the meat.
- Never cover roasting meat with a lid or foil. It will produce steam and the meat will be an anaemic colour, with a dull taste and stringy texture.
- Boneless beef filets and ribeye roasts are tender, tubular pieces of meat that cook in a flash. Because of their shape, the thickness of the meat determines the cooking time, not the weight. Measure the meat vertically at its thickest point and roast at 450 F for 15 minutes per inch for rare; 20 minutes per inch for medium-rare; 25 minutes per inch for medium to well done.
- Although not foolproof, a roast's cooking time can be estimated by weight. In general, using the high heat roasting method, cook for 15 minutes per pound with an extra 15 minutes for rare, or 20 minutes per pound with an extra 20 minutes for medium.
- Let the meat sit, loosely covered with a tea towel, for 10 minutes before carving, to allow the juices to retract. The roast will be easier to carve.
- An instant-read thermometer will confirm that your meat is cooked. At the end of the cooking time, stick the thermometer into the fleshiest part of the meat and withdraw as soon as the needle stops going up. Roast to 125 F for rare, 140 F for medium rare and 160 F for well done.

If your roast is too rare in the middle, slice it up and slip the underdone slices into the gravy while it is simmering on the stove.

Horseradish-crusted Beef Filet

SERVES 6

Serve the filet on its own or drizzled with the soy balsamic syrup. Stir-fried bok choy and shiitake mushrooms and coconut-flavoured mashed potatoes are great accompaniments.

3 tbsp olive oil	½ cup prepared horseradish, well drained
1 beef filet (about 3 lb/1.5 kg)	½ cup panko or dry breadcrumbs
2 tbsp wasabi paste	Salt and freshly ground pepper
2 tbsp soy sauce	

HEAT 1 tbsp oil in a large skillet over high heat. Add filet and sear for about 2 minutes per side (about 8 minutes in total), or until golden. Remove from heat.

COMBINE wasabi, soy sauce and 1 tbsp oil in a small bowl. Brush over filet.

COMBINE horseradish, panko and remaining 1 tbsp oil in a bowl. Pat over meat. Season with salt and pepper. Marinate for 30 minutes.

PREHEAT oven to 450 F.

PLACE meat on a rack in a roasting pan. Roast for 40 to 45 minutes (depending on thickness), or until an instant-read thermometer reads 125 F for rare, or until done to taste. Remove roast to a carving board to rest for 10 minutes before carving.

{ soy balsamic syrup }

This syrup is wonderful with grilled dishes, or use it just to make a plate look pretty. It keeps in the refrigerator for months.

In a small pot, combine ½ cup granulated sugar, ½ cup water, ½ cup balsamic vinegar, ¼ cup soy sauce, 3 peeled and halved shallots, ½ tsp chili flakes and 3 star anise.

Bring to a boil and boil for 7 minutes, or until slightly thickened. Strain and reheat when needed.

Makes about ¾ cup.

{ squeeze bottles }

Restaurant chefs keep syrups and infused oils in squeeze bottles to give the plate a finished look. Drizzle the syrup around food or in decorative lines on a plate. The effect is so impressive that people will think there is a professional hiding in the kitchen!

Barbecued Beef Brisket

SERVES 6 TO 8

This brisket is simmered in a barbecue-type sauce until it is meltingly tender. Leftovers make great sandwiches. I like to make it ahead of time and refrigerate it so it is easier to skim off the fat before reheating. Remove the fat, bring the sauce to a boil and reduce if necessary.

My friend Mary Ellen Herman adds soaked dried lima beans to the sauce before cooking, plus 2 extra cups of water for a deluxe version of baked beans. Or for pulled pork substitute a boned pork shoulder for the brisket and, when cool, pull it apart with a fork.

2 cups pureed canned tomatoes
1 cup beef or chicken stock
1/4 cup white vinegar
2 tbsp brown sugar
1 tbsp Worcestershire sauce
1 tbsp chili powder

1 tsp smoked paprika
Salt and freshly ground pepper
2 tbsp vegetable oil
1 beef brisket (about 5 lb/2 kg)
4 cups chopped onions
2 tbsp sliced garlic

COMBINE tomatoes, stock, vinegar, sugar, Worcestershire, chili powder, paprika, salt and pepper in a bowl. Reserve.

HEAT oil in a heavy casserole over medium-high heat. Season brisket with salt and pepper and brown it well on all sides, about 3 minutes per side. Remove from casserole.

PREHEAT oven to 300 F.

REDUCE heat to medium-low. Add onions to casserole and sauté gently for 6 minutes. Add garlic and cook for 4 minutes longer, or until vegetables are softened.

RETURN brisket to casserole and pour sauce mixture over top. Bake, covered, turning and basting occasionally, for 3 to 3½ hours, or until brisket is fork-tender.

REMOVE meat from casserole and skim any fat from sauce. Boil sauce over high heat for a few minutes, or until sauce has reduced by one-third and thickened slightly. Slice meat against grain and reheat in sauce.

{ brisket }

You can buy double or single briskets. A double brisket is fattier, juicier and has more flavour. I would recommend it, especially if you are cooking the brisket ahead. Chill the meat and sauce and remove the fat after it has congealed.

Argentinean Grilled Beef

SERVES 4

In this recipe, the often chewy flank steak is tenderized and given a burst of flavour with a herbal, citrus marinade. Serve the beef with the spicy Argentinean salsa.

1 flank steak (about 1 1/2 lb/750 g)	1/2 cup orange juice
1 tbsp chopped fresh coriander	1 tbsp lime juice
1 tbsp chopped fresh basil	1 tsp hot Asian chili sauce
1 tbsp chopped fresh mint	3 tbsp olive oil
2 tsp finely chopped garlic	Salt and freshly ground pepper

PLACE steak in a baking dish or plastic bag. Combine coriander, basil, mint, garlic, orange juice, lime juice, chili sauce and 2 tbsp oil. Pour over steak and marinate for 2 hours or overnight in refrigerator.

REMOVE steak from marinade and pat dry. Brush with remaining 1 tbsp oil.

PREHEAT grill or broiler on high. Season steak with salt and pepper. Grill for about 4 minutes per side, or until steak is medium-rare.

CARVE steak against grain into slices 1/2 inch thick.

{ argentinean salsa }

This fresh-tasting, herbal hot sauce is sometimes called chimichurri. It can
take many different forms, but my version has a pesto-like texture and is not as hot as many others. Heat it up with more chilies, if desired. It is excellent with plain meat, chicken or fish. Combined with some sour cream, it also makes a great dip.

In a food processor, combine 1/4 cup olive oil, 2 tbsp red wine vinegar, 1 tbsp lime juice, 1 tsp chopped garlic, 1 cup chopped green onions, 1/2 cup chopped fresh coriander, 1/2 cup chopped parsley and 2 tbsp seeded and chopped jalapeño. Process until combined but still with a bit of texture. Season with salt and pepper.

Makes about 1 1/2 cups.

Grilled Ribeyes

SERVES 4

Excellent steaks begin with great meat. If the meat is good, salt and pepper are enough seasoning. Or, to heighten the flavour, use a barbecue rub or serve the steaks with a flavoured butter.

Ribeyes—the centre of a rib steak without the bone—have great flavour and texture. My son-in-law Shane is a barbecue maven, and this is his favourite steak. Try serving it with a pat of peppercorn butter.

4 ribeye steaks, about 1 ½ inches thick
1 tbsp olive oil
Salt and freshly ground pepper

BRUSH steaks with oil. Season with salt and pepper just before grilling.

PREHEAT grill on high. Grill steaks for 4 minutes with lid closed. Turn and continue to grill for 4 to 5 minutes for medium-rare, or until done to taste. Salt again before serving.

{ peppercorn butter }

In a food processor, coarsely chop 2 tsp each black, white and green peppercorns and 1 tsp coriander seeds. Add ½ cup butter and process until combined. Place butter on a sheet of plastic wrap and roll into a log. Refrigerate for up to a week and then freeze if not used. Cut into slices and serve on steak.

Makes about ½ cup.

{ steaks for the grill }

Flat-iron, hanger and tri-tip steaks are the new darlings of the lean steak set. The flat-iron steak is also known as top blade. It is very tender and flavourful, with a texture like beef filet. The hanger steak is a favourite in France, where it is known as onglet; it is the traditional steak in steak frites. It comes from underneath the filet and has quite a coarse grain. Tri-tip is the bottom end of the sirloin. It has a triangular shape and can be cut into steaks or cooked as one piece. It also braises well.

All three steaks grill very easily. Hanger and flat-iron steaks take about 4 to 5 minutes a side; the thicker tri-tip takes about 7 minutes a side. I usually sprinkle the steaks with a dry rub, or you can marinate them in your favourite marinade or barbecue sauce for about 4 hours in the refrigerator. All these steaks must be carved against the grain.

Beef Ribs

SERVES 6

These are my favourite ribs, and this recipe has been satisfying my family for years. Double the sauce if you want extra for dipping. The ribs are cut from rib roasts and are sold in a rack or already cut into individual ribs. If you buy individual ribs, reduce the cooking time by 5 minutes.

¼ cup Dijon mustard	1 tbsp chopped garlic
¼ cup olive oil	2 tsp paprika
¼ cup balsamic vinegar	2 tsp dried thyme
2 tbsp soy sauce	4 racks beef ribs
1 tbsp chili powder	Salt

COMBINE mustard, oil, vinegar, soy sauce, chili powder, garlic, paprika and thyme. Brush over ribs. Marinate for 2 to 12 hours, refrigerated.

PREHEAT grill on high. Grill ribs for about 10 minutes per side, or until meat is slightly pink, brushing occasionally with marinade. (Alternatively, roast ribs in a 450 F oven for 20 minutes, or until browned and crisp but still a little rare.) Salt to taste.

{ homemade barbecue rub }

Make this in quantity and keep it on hand to flavour any grilled steak. Rub it over the meat before grilling.

Combine 1 tbsp paprika, 1 tbsp chili powder, 1 tsp dry mustard, 1 tsp dried thyme, 1 tsp kosher salt and ½ tsp freshly ground pepper. Keeps in a cupboard for about 6 months.

Makes about ¼ cup.

Roasted Tuscan Steak

SERVES 4

Rib steaks are my favourite cut. They are especially adaptable to roasting, and a single thick steak is perfect for two people. In this recipe, the meat is seared and then roasted for a short time. Slice it thinly and serve it on a bed of arugula with some good salt. It's like a little roast beef for two.

2 tbsp olive oil
2 rib steaks, about 2 inches thick
Salt and freshly ground pepper
1 cup finely chopped red onions
1 tbsp finely chopped garlic

$1/4$ cup chopped parsley
1 tsp grated lemon rind
1 bunch arugula
1 tbsp fleur de sel, Maldon or kosher salt

PREHEAT oven to 450 F.

HEAT oil in a large skillet over high heat. Season steaks with salt and pepper. Fry steaks for 2 minutes per side, or until browned.

TRANSFER steaks to a baking sheet and roast for 10 minutes. Turn and roast for 8 to 10 minutes longer, or until medium-rare. (Roast for an additional 10 minutes for medium to well done.)

COMBINE onions, garlic, parsley and lemon rind in a small bowl while steaks are roasting.

DIVIDE arugula among 4 serving plates. Carve steak into thin slices and fan over arugula. Sprinkle with onion mixture and fleur de sel.

{ fleur de sel }

Fleur de sel is a French sea salt that incorporates the flavours of the sea and many mineral elements. It is not too salty and finishes dishes to perfection. Because of its expense, it is only used for garnishing food, never for cooking. I actually prefer the less expensive Maldon salt from the English coast. Its flakes look like Ivory Snow, and they melt onto the meat. Failing this, use kosher or sea salt.

Malaysian Stir-fry of Beef, Leeks, Mushrooms and Beans

SERVES 4

Malaysian food is steeped in history, reflecting the cultures that have occupied the country at different times. Because of this, Indian and Chinese cuisines heavily influence Malay cooking, and this recipe combines these cross-cultural ingredients in an outstanding stir-fry. Serve it with rice.

New York sirloin is a boneless cut, more tender than top sirloin.

1 lb (500 g) New York sirloin, trimmed	1 tsp chopped garlic
2 tbsp Indian curry paste	Salt and freshly ground pepper
2 tbsp soy sauce	1 cup chopped leeks
1 tbsp hoisin sauce	8 oz (250 g) large mushrooms, quartered
2 tbsp vegetable oil	4 oz (125 g) green beans, trimmed and cut in 2-inch pieces
1 tbsp chopped gingerroot	1/2 red onion, thinly sliced

CUT steak into 1-inch cubes and place in a large bowl.

COMBINE curry paste, soy sauce, hoisin and 1 tbsp oil in a small bowl. Toss meat with half the marinade and marinate for 1 hour.

HEAT a wok or skillet over high heat. Add remaining 1 tbsp oil and heat. Add ginger and garlic and stir-fry for 30 seconds.

DRAIN beef and season with salt and pepper. Add beef to wok in batches so as not to crowd pan. Stir-fry for about 2 minutes, or until meat is browned on outside but still rare inside. Transfer meat to a bowl with a slotted spoon.

ADD leeks, mushrooms and green beans to wok and stir-fry for 3 minutes, or until softened. Stir in reserved marinade. Add reserved meat and any juices and stir to combine. Cook for 2 minutes, or until meat is hot.

SERVE garnished with sliced red onions.

Mediterranean Shortribs

SERVES 6

A wonderfully aromatic braise with an Eastern Mediterranean flavour. Shortribs are my favourite cut to stew. The bones add flavour and the meat stays juicy. I find that baking the ribs without any sauce at the end improves the texture, but you can omit this step.

Make this a day ahead. After they have been refrigerated it is easy to remove the fat. The taste also improves as the shortribs marinate in the sauce.

2 tbsp ground coriander	2 cups chopped onions
2 tbsp ground cumin	1 cup red wine
1 tbsp freshly ground pepper	1 tsp dried thyme
2 tsp ground fennel seeds	3 cups beef stock
6 racks shortribs, about 1 ½ inches thick	12 whole peeled garlic cloves
Salt	18 pitted green olives
3 tbsp olive oil	

PREHEAT oven to 300 F.

COMBINE coriander, cumin, pepper and fennel in a small bowl. Rub ribs with half the spice mixture. Season ribs with salt.

HEAT 2 tbsp oil in a skillet over medium-high heat. Brown shortribs, in batches, for about 2 minutes per side. Transfer to a casserole.

POUR off fat, wipe out skillet and add remaining 1 tbsp oil. Reduce heat to medium-low.

ADD onions to skillet and cook for 10 minutes, or until very soft and slightly browned.

ADD reserved spice mixture and sauté for 1 minute. Add wine and bring to a boil. Add thyme and stock and return to a boil.

POUR sauce over shortribs. Bake, covered, for 1 hour. Add garlic and bake for 30 minutes longer. Add olives and bake for 45 minutes, or until meat is very tender.

REMOVE meat from sauce and place on a baking sheet. Skim fat from sauce. Increase oven temperature to 400 F. Bake shortribs for 15 minutes to brown them. Return ribs to sauce (remove meat from bones if preferred) and reheat.

Burgundian Beef Burgers with Brie

SERVES 4

This burger came out of a session I did with student chefs from George Brown College in Toronto. I asked them to come up with a burger for my column, and this recipe received many plaudits from readers. The burger has a rich flavour and is very juicy, even when you cook it medium. Serve it with Dijon mustard on your favourite bread or bun (they are especially good on cheese buns). Substitute any cheese for the Brie, if desired.

1 tsp olive oil	1 egg, beaten
4 slices bacon, finely chopped	Salt and freshly ground pepper
¼ cup finely chopped shallots	1 lb (500 g) ground beef
2 cups finely chopped mushrooms	4 oz (125 g) Brie
1 tsp Worcestershire sauce	4 hamburger buns

HEAT oil in a skillet over medium heat and sauté bacon until just cooked but not crispy, about 5 minutes.

ADD shallots and cook until translucent, about 2 minutes. Add mushrooms and cook until water evaporates, about 2 minutes. Transfer to a large bowl and let cool.

ADD Worcestershire, egg, salt and pepper to mushroom mixture. Add beef and use your hands or a spatula to incorporate gently without overmixing.

SHAPE meat mixture into 8 patties about ½ inch thick.

CUT Brie into 4 slices. Sandwich a piece of Brie between two patties, encasing cheese to prevent any leakage. You should have 4 patties about 1 inch thick.

PREHEAT grill on high. Grill patties with lid closed for 4 minutes per side, or until patties are cooked to taste. Serve on buns.

{ grilling and barbecuing }

Grilling and barbecuing refer to cooking over direct heat. Traditionally, barbecuing meant cooking meat over slow, low heat for several hours, whereas grilling meant fast cooking over high heat. But today the terms are used interchangeably.

If you don't have a barbecue, you can use a grill pan—a ridged skillet made of heavy metal—on the stove (usually a better method than broiling, because the hot grill sears the meat). When using a barbecue, grill with the lid closed.

{ crisp onion rings }

These are best eaten as soon as they are made, but you can also make them ahead and reheat at 400 F for 3 minutes.

Combine 1½ cups buttermilk, ¼ tsp cayenne (or more to taste) and 2 thinly sliced sweet onions in a bowl. Let sit for 15 minutes.

Combine 1 cup all-purpose flour, salt and pepper on a plate.

Remove onions from buttermilk with tongs. Toss onions in flour until lightly coated.

Heat about 2 inches vegetable oil in a wok or skillet to 350 F, or until a cube of bread turns brown in 15 seconds. Fry rings, in batches, for about 2 minutes, or until golden. Drain on paper towels.

Serves 4.

{ chili fries }

Scrub 4 large Yukon Gold or baking potatoes. Cut potatoes in half and cut each half into three wedges. Toss with 2 tbsp chili powder, 3 tbsp olive oil and salt. Spread on a baking sheet and bake in a preheated 400 F oven for 25 minutes. Turn and bake for 10 minutes longer, or until browned and tender.

Serves 4.

{ barbecued french fries }

Quick and easy French fries without deep-frying. Make lots, as everyone loves them.

Peel 1½ lb (750 g) Yukon Gold potatoes and cut into thin French fries about ¼ inch thick. Spread in a single layer in a metal baking pan and toss with ⅓ cup vegetable oil and salt. Cover with foil.

Preheat grill on high and grill potatoes for 10 minutes, shaking dish occasionally. Remove foil and cook for 3 to 5 minutes longer, or until fries are crisp. Drain well.

Serves 6.

Braised Beef Italian Style

SERVES 4

This rich beef braise makes a good family dinner. Serve it with pasta or rice on the side.

2 tbsp olive oil	1 tsp chopped garlic
1 ½ lb (750 g) stewing beef, cut in 2-inch pieces	1 cup red wine
Salt and freshly ground pepper	2 tsp chopped fresh rosemary, or ½ tsp dried
¼ cup diced pancetta	1 cup beef or chicken stock
1 cup chopped onions	2 cups chopped canned or fresh tomatoes
½ cup chopped carrots	1 bay leaf

PREHEAT oven to 325 F.

HEAT oil in a skillet over medium-high heat. Pat beef dry and season with salt and pepper. Add beef to skillet in batches and sear until browned, about 1 minute per side. Transfer beef to a casserole.

REDUCE heat to medium-low. Add pancetta and cook until golden, about 2 minutes. Add onions and carrots and cook for 2 minutes, or until softened. Add garlic and cook for 1 more minute.

ADD wine and rosemary and bring to a boil, scraping up any caramelized bits on bottom of pan. Add stock, tomatoes and bay leaf. Bring to a boil. Transfer contents to casserole.

BAKE, covered, for 2 hours, or until meat is tender. Cool. Skim off any fat and remove bay leaf. Reheat when needed.

{ pancetta }

Pancetta is unsmoked Italian bacon that is cured with salt and spices. It is made from the pork belly and after curing is rolled into a salami-like roll. You could use bacon instead, but there is no real substitute.

The dishes of the people—peasant food—are all stews, whether it is a curry from India, beef braised in red wine from France, chicken bathed in soy sauce from China or osso bucco from Italy.

Braising and stewing are interchangeable terms. Both mean long, slow cooking in liquid, although traditionally braising was done on a bed of finely chopped vegetables, while stewing was not. Both braising and stewing are usually done in the oven because the heat is more even.

BASIC BRAISING OR STEWING TIPS

- Tougher cuts are often best for stewing, because they have more flavour and texture than tender cuts, and long, slow cooking in liquid makes them tender. Don't be misled; more expensive meat does not mean better stews. The best cuts for stewing are beef chuck, shoulder, shank and shortribs; veal shoulder and breast; pork butt, shoulder and leg; lamb shoulder, shank and breast; older poultry, preferably hens; thicker fish such as monkfish, grouper, halibut or squid.

- Trim most of the fat from the meat, then either leave the meat whole or cut it into uniform pieces (usually 1- to 2-inch cubes) for even cooking. If you are stewing vegetables, they should be the same size whatever one chooses.

- Use a heavy pot or a Dutch oven that can be used on top of the stove and in the oven. A tight-fitting lid is essential to prevent the liquid from evaporating. Failing this, brown the meat in a skillet and then transfer to a casserole to finish the cooking in the oven.

- For the most successful stews, use the right-sized baking dish. Cubed stewing meat should sit in two layers, while one piece of meat should fit snugly inside the casserole. Too large a casserole causes the gravy to evaporate too quickly; too small means the meat can cook unevenly.

- Brown the meat before braising to seal in the juices. It is not necessary to dust the meat with flour, but make sure the meat is dry (pat it dry with paper towels).

- After browning, use gentle heat to cook the meat slowly—300 to 325 F is perfect for stews. Turning up the heat will not make the stew cook more quickly, and it will toughen the fibres of the meat.

- Meat is cooked when it can be easily pierced with a fork—usually about 2 hours for beef, 1½ hours for lamb and pork and 1 hour for chicken (depending on its age). Fish stews usually cook for only about 20 minutes.

Lemon-scented Roast Lamb

SERVES 6

Cooking a leg of lamb on the bone helps to keep the meat juicy. Have the butcher crack the shank bone, so it can be cut off as a treat for the bone lover.

1 lamb leg, trimmed (about 5 lb/2.5 kg)	Salt
2 tbsp chopped fresh rosemary, or 2 tsp dried	1/2 cup red wine
1 tbsp chopped garlic	1 tbsp balsamic vinegar
1 tbsp grated lemon rind	2 cups beef stock
1 tbsp cracked black peppercorns	2 tbsp red currant jelly
1/4 cup olive oil	Fresh rosemary sprigs

PLACE lamb in a large dish. Combine rosemary, garlic, lemon rind, pepper and oil in a small bowl. Brush mixture on lamb and let marinate for 2 hours or overnight in refrigerator.

PREHEAT oven to 400 F.

PLACE lamb on a rack in a roasting pan. Season with salt. Roast for 1 hour and 30 minutes, or until lamb juices run pink at thickest part of leg. Baste occasionally during roasting.

PREPARE sauce while lamb is roasting by combining wine and vinegar in a small pot. Bring to a boil and boil for 6 minutes, or until reduced to a glaze (mixture should coat back of a spoon). Add stock and boil for 10 minutes, or until reduced by half.

REMOVE lamb from oven and let rest on a carving board for 10 minutes.

POUR off any fat from roasting pan. Add sauce to pan and bring to a boil over medium heat, stirring up caramelized bits on bottom of pan. Reduce heat to low and whisk in red currant jelly.

CARVE lamb into thin slices. Drizzle sauce around plates and garnish with rosemary sprigs.

{ lamb }

Canadians used to resist buying lamb, but consumption is increasing as lamb farming improves. Canadian lamb is now a viable alternative to beef.

We can also buy frozen (and occasionally fresh) New Zealand lamb, which is generally milder in flavour than Canadian lamb. Defrost frozen lamb for 24 hours in the refrigerator for minimum flavour loss.

- Lamb legs are tender and delicately flavoured. They are best roasted or barbecued. For the best texture and flavour, buy legs that are no larger than 6 pounds. Cook bone-in lamb at 400 F for 15 minutes per pound plus an extra 15 minutes; boneless lamb takes about 30 to 35 minutes in total for medium-rare.
- To butterfly a lamb leg, have the butcher remove the bone and slice the leg open. The butcher may also remove the fell—the layer of skin that turns into crisp crackling, but you can cut it away yourself using a small sharp knife.
- Lamb chops are tender and can be grilled or fried. Rib chops correspond to beef rib steaks. Loin chops look like a tiny porterhouse steaks. If the bone is removed and the nugget of meat is tied in a circle, it is called a noisette. Look for chops that are at least 1 inch thick for the best texture and flavour.
- Boneless lamb loins offer excellent eating as well as value for money. They are available fresh at upscale butchers or frozen at the supermarket.
- Lamb rack is the first eight chops of the rib section, sold in one piece. The rack is roasted whole and then sliced into chops for serving. Two or three racks tied together are called a crown roast.
- Lamb shoulder is fatty but has excellent flavour and texture. It should be boned before cooking, because the configuration of the bones makes it very difficult to carve. Shoulders are either braised or roasted. They can also be cut up into stewing lamb.
- Lamb shanks are exceptionally tasty and feature on many restaurant menus. They are braised slowly for a long time to break down the connective tissue. Buy one per person.

{ carving a leg of lamb }

Hold the leg firmly with the back of a carving fork (so as not to pierce the meat). Cut ½-inch slices perpendicular to the bone from the shank (narrow) end. Then cut parallel to the bone to release the slices. Turn the leg over and carve the other side.

Barbecued Lamb Provençal

SERVES 6

A boned and butterflied leg of lamb is quite uneven in thickness, which means some pieces will be better done and some rarer, pleasing everyone.

In this recipe the anchovies disappear in the marinade, leaving a mysterious background taste that people love. Serve this with rouille, a spicy red pepper mayonnaise.

1 butterflied leg of lamb (about 3 to 4 lb/1.5 to 2 kg after boning)	2 tsp chopped garlic
¼ cup olive oil	2 tbsp fresh chopped rosemary, or 2 tsp dried
¼ cup lemon juice	2 tbsp chopped fresh basil
2 tbsp Dijon mustard	½ tsp cayenne
3 anchovy fillets, chopped	1 bay leaf

PLACE lamb in a large dish. Combine oil, lemon juice, mustard, anchovies, garlic, rosemary, basil, cayenne and bay leaf in a bowl. Pour over lamb and marinate for 12 hours, refrigerated. Remove lamb from marinade.

PREHEAT grill on high. Turn off one burner and place lamb on that side, fat side down. Cook for 15 minutes with the lid closed. Turn and cook for 15 to 20 minutes, or until meat is medium-rare. If grill flares up, douse flames with water.

CUT lamb into three pieces along natural breaks and carve each piece against grain into thin slices.

{ rouille }

Cut 2 red peppers and 1 jalapeño in half and remove seeds and ribs. Place cut side down on a baking sheet and bake at 425 F for 15 minutes. Remove jalapeño and continue to cook red peppers for 15 minutes, or until skin blisters.

Cool peppers and peel. (Alternatively, buy 2 roasted peppers and add 1 tsp hot Asian chili sauce.)

In a food processor or blender, combine peppers, 1 tsp chopped garlic, ½ cup mayonnaise, 1 tbsp lemon juice and 1 tbsp olive oil. Process until smooth. Season with salt and pepper.

Makes about 1¼ cups.

Sosatie

SERVES 4

Sosatie means "meat on a stick" in South Africa, where this recipe originates. It is a spicy marinated lamb grilled on skewers with apricots and onions. Use metal skewers or soaked wooden ones.

1/2 cup chopped onions	2 tbsp red wine vinegar
1 tbsp chopped gingerroot	1/2 cup red wine
1/2 tsp chopped garlic	1 1/2 lb (750 g) boneless leg of lamb,
1 tbsp Indian curry paste	cut in 1-inch cubes
1 1/2 tsp brown sugar	8 shallots or small onions, peeled
1 tsp whole coriander seeds	16 dried apricots
1/2 tsp ground turmeric	2 tbsp vegetable oil
2 tbsp apricot jam	Salt and freshly ground pepper

COMBINE chopped onions, ginger, garlic, curry paste, sugar, coriander, turmeric and jam in a food processor and process until pasty. Add vinegar and wine and process until fairly smooth.

PLACE lamb, shallots and apricots in a baking dish. Add marinade and toss. Marinate for 12 hours, refrigerated.

PREHEAT grill on medium-high.

THREAD meat, apricots and shallots on skewers. Brush with oil and season with salt and pepper. Grill for about 2 minutes per side, for a total of 8 minutes.

PLACE remaining marinade in a small pot and bring to a boil. Boil until thickened, about 1 minute. Serve sauce on the side.

Rack of Lamb with Arugula and Mint Vinaigrette

SERVES 4

A simple but delightful dish for easy entertaining. Ask the butcher to clean the fat from the bones. You can omit the pomegranate juice and seeds if desired, but the seeds look beautiful and add crunch to the dish.

2 tbsp butter, softened	1 tbsp balsamic vinegar
1/2 tsp finely chopped garlic	Salt
1 tsp grated lime rind	1 tbsp pomegranate juice
1 tbsp lime juice	3 tbsp olive oil
1/4 cup chopped fresh mint	2 bunches arugula, trimmed
Freshly ground pepper	1/2 cup pomegranate seeds
2 lamb racks	

BEAT butter, garlic, lime rind, lime juice, 2 tbsp mint and pepper in a small bowl. Spread over lamb racks. Marinate for 30 minutes.

PREHEAT oven to 400 F.

SALT lamb and place on a rack in a roasting pan. Roast for 30 to 45 minutes, or until juices run pink. Let lamb rest for 5 minutes.

WHISK vinegar, pomegranate juice, oil and remaining 2 tbsp mint in a large bowl. Add arugula and toss well. Divide arugula among serving plates.

SLICE lamb rack into chops. Serve lamb on a bed of arugula and scatter with pomegranate seeds. Pour any accumulated juices over chops.

{ salting meat }

Using salt properly is very important in cooking; salt brings out the flavour, but it must be used judiciously so that it doesn't overwhelm the dish. Always salt meat, poultry and fish just before you cook it because salt draws out the juices; but when reducing a sauce, always salt to taste afterwards. In cooking, I always use coarse grained kosher salt because it is additive-free, flakey and melts more easily on food.

Lamb Chops from Fez

SERVES 4

Serve harissa—a spicy chili-laden Moroccan sauce—on the side or use Asian chili sauce as a substitute. Substitute flank steak for the lamb chops if desired, and grill for 4 minutes per side.

Serve this with Israeli couscous (page 181).

1 tbsp finely chopped garlic	1 tsp ground cumin
1 tbsp lemon juice	2 tbsp olive oil
1 tbsp finely chopped parsley	12 lamb rib chops, 1 inch thick, trimmed
1 tbsp finely chopped fresh coriander	Salt and freshly ground pepper

COMBINE garlic, lemon juice, parsley, coriander, cumin and 1 tbsp oil in a bowl. Brush on both sides of lamb chops and season with salt and pepper. Marinate for 15 minutes.

PREHEAT oven to 400 F.

HEAT remaining tbsp oil in a large skillet over medium-high heat. Add chops in batches and sear for about 1 minute per side (including fat side). Transfer to a baking sheet and bake for 5 to 7 minutes for medium-rare, or until cooked to desired degree of doneness.

{ harissa }

The heat of this sauce depends on the heat of the chilies. If you want it even hotter, add cayenne to taste. The sauce will keep, refrigerated, for up to a month.

Quarter, seed and stem 4 dried chili peppers (such as ancho). Soak chilies and 2 tsp dried mint in hot water for 30 minutes, or until softened. Drain through a sieve.

Add 4 peeled garlic cloves, 2 tsp coriander seeds, 2 tsp caraway seeds and 1 tsp cumin seeds through feed tube of a food processor with machine running. Add chilies, mint and 2 tbsp olive oil and puree until smooth.

Makes about ¾ cup.

Fiery Lamb T-bones with Roasted Tomato Sauce

SERVES 4

Lamb T-bones are loin chops with the tenderloin attached. Ask the butcher to cut them 2 inches thick.

2 tbsp hot pepper sauce	**Roasted Tomato Sauce**
2 tbsp mint chutney or mint sauce	4 plum tomatoes, halved and seeded
1 tbsp honey	1 red onion, peeled and cut in 8 wedges
1 tsp finely chopped garlic	6 sprigs rosemary
1 tbsp olive oil	1 tbsp olive oil
8 lamb loin chops	Salt and freshly ground pepper
	1 cup chicken or beef stock
	1 tbsp balsamic vinegar
	Salt and freshly ground pepper

COMBINE hot sauce, chutney, honey, garlic and oil. Brush over chops and marinate for at least 1 hour.

PREPARE sauce while lamb is marinating. Combine tomatoes, onion, rosemary, oil, salt and pepper in a bowl. Spread on a baking sheet and bake for 25 minutes, or until onions are brown and tomatoes are soft.

CHOP onions and tomatoes. Transfer to a pot and add stock. Bring to a boil and cook until sauce-like, about 3 to 5 minutes. Stir in vinegar. Season with salt and pepper.

PREHEAT oven to 425 F.

HEAT a large skillet over medium-high heat. Holding chops with tongs, fry fat side down for 1 minute, or until fat starts to colour. Continue to fry chops for 1 minute per side, or until golden. Transfer chops to a baking sheet.

BAKE chops for 5 minutes. Turn chops and bake for 5 to 6 minutes longer, or until cooked but still pink inside. Serve chops topped with sauce.

Classic Braised Lamb Shanks

SERVES 4

These are the best lamb shanks ever, according to my husband, Bruce, the lamb-shank expert in our family. They are slow cooked and end up richly glazed with sauce.

2 tbsp vegetable oil	3 cups beef stock
4 lamb shanks	2 tbsp balsamic vinegar
2 tsp chopped fresh rosemary, or 1 tsp dried	1 tsp granulated sugar
Salt and freshly ground pepper	2 tbsp tomato paste
1 cup chopped onions	1 bay leaf
1 tsp chopped garlic	1 strip orange rind (about 1 inch wide)
2 tbsp all-purpose flour	2 tbsp chopped parsley
½ cup red wine	

PREHEAT oven to 300 F.

HEAT oil in a large casserole over medium-high heat. Sprinkle lamb shanks with 1 tsp rosemary and season with salt and pepper. Brown shanks on all sides, about 2 minutes per side, or until a dark brown colour. Remove from casserole.

REDUCE heat to medium-low. Add onions and garlic to casserole and sauté until softened, about 5 minutes. Sprinkle with flour and cook, stirring, for 2 minutes, or until flour has browned slightly.

ADD wine and bring to a boil, stirring. Add stock, vinegar, sugar, tomato paste, bay leaf, orange rind and remaining 1 tsp rosemary. Bring to a boil. Return shanks to casserole.

COVER and bake for 1 hour and 15 minutes, turning once. Uncover and continue to bake for 30 minutes, turning once, until lamb is very tender and sauce is thick and rich. Remove bay leaf and orange rind before serving. Sprinkle with parsley.

{ parsley }

I always use flat-leafed Italian parsley. It has a stronger, sweeter flavour and is easier to chop than curly parsley. It is often available at the supermarket but can also be easily grown in a garden or window box. Remove any thick stems before chopping.

New Irish Stew

SERVES 6 TO 8

Time is always a consideration for me, so here is a mouth-watering, contemporary version of Irish stew made with ground lamb layered with red potatoes (they have less starch and hold their shape better than Yukon Golds).

1 tbsp vegetable oil	1 tbsp Dijon mustard
1 Spanish onion, halved and thinly sliced	Salt and freshly ground pepper
2 lb (1 kg) ground lamb	3 lb (1.5 kg) red potatoes, thinly sliced
1 tbsp chopped fresh rosemary, or 1 tsp dried	4 garlic cloves, thinly sliced
1/2 cup red wine	2 tbsp butter
2 cups chopped canned tomatoes	1 cup grated Cheddar cheese
1 tbsp Worcestershire sauce	

PREHEAT oven to 375 F.

HEAT oil in a large skillet over medium heat. Add onions and sauté for 5 minutes. Remove from skillet and reserve.

ADD lamb and sauté until it loses its pinkness, about 5 minutes. Add rosemary, wine, tomatoes, Worcestershire and mustard. Bring to a boil, reduce heat and simmer for 10 minutes, or until sauce has reduced and thickened slightly. Taste for seasoning, adding salt and pepper as needed.

TOSS potato slices with salt and pepper. In a buttered casserole, layer one-third of the potatoes, half the garlic, half the onions and half the lamb. Add one-third more potatoes, then remaining garlic, onions and lamb. Finish with remaining potatoes and dot with butter.

BAKE, covered, for 30 minutes. Uncover, sprinkle with cheese and bake for 30 minutes longer, or until potatoes are tender.

{ cooking with herbs }

Fresh herbs add excellent flavour to all dishes, but they are not always available. If you substitute dried herbs, use one-third the amount (e.g., 1 tbsp chopped fresh rosemary = 1 tsp dried).

Sweetly Spiced Pork with Honey and Sherry Vinegar

SERVES 4

This cinnamon and coriander dusting is scrumptious. Cook the pork until it is still slightly pink so it stays juicy and tender.

2 pork tenderloins (each cut in 4 pieces)	$1/2$ cup red wine
2 tsp ground cinnamon	$1/4$ cup sherry vinegar
2 tsp ground coriander	1 tsp honey
Salt and freshly ground pepper	1 cup chicken stock
2 tbsp olive oil	

PREHEAT oven to 425 F.

SEASON pork with cinnamon, coriander, salt and pepper.

HEAT oil in a large ovenproof skillet over medium-high heat. Fry pork for 1 to 2 minutes per side, or until browned.

TRANSFER skillet to oven and cook for 5 to 8 minutes (end pieces take less time than middle pieces), or until pork is cooked through but still slightly pink in centre.

TRANSFER pork to a plate and cover to keep warm.

RETURN skillet to stove over medium-high heat. Add wine, vinegar and honey. Bring to a boil and cook for 5 minutes, or until syrupy, stirring to scrape any brown bits from bottom of pan. Add stock and boil until sauce begins to thicken, about 4 minutes. Serve sauce over pork.

{ pork }

I remember the days when pork was dry and tasteless, with a texture like shoe leather. For many years farmers bred pork to be lean to satisfy the consumer's desire for less-fatty products, but at the expense of taste and texture. Now there has been a revolution in breeding methods and farm practices, and pork has become far more popular, both in restaurants and at home. Organic and naturally raised pork are available at organic supermarkets and good butchers. Farmers are also returning to old breeds like Berkshire and Tamworth (sometimes called heritage pork), which are fattier and tastier.

Today it is quite safe to cook pork slightly underdone for the best flavour and texture.

Pork Finished with a Shower of Clams

SERVES 6

This is a somewhat upmarket version of a traditional Portuguese dish. Try to get the end piece of the pork loin, as it has a bit more fat. You can prepare the sauce ahead of time. Reheat it, add the clams and cooked pork, and dinner is ready.

1 garlic head, separated into cloves	1 cup diced onions
2 tbsp chopped fresh coriander	1/2 cup diced celery
1/4 cup chopped parsley	1 red pepper, seeded and diced
1/2 cup olive oil	1 tsp chili flakes
Salt and freshly ground pepper	1/2 cup white wine
1 1/2 lb (750 g) boneless pork loin, cubed	1 cup chopped canned tomatoes
1/2 cup chopped chorizo or other smoked sausage	2 lb (1 kg) fresh clams

PLACE garlic cloves in a small pot, cover with water, bring to a boil and simmer for 10 minutes, or until garlic is very soft. Drain. Peel garlic.

COMBINE garlic, 1 tbsp coriander, 2 tbsp parsley, 1/4 cup oil, salt and pepper in a food processor and puree until smooth.

TOSS pork and garlic paste in a large bowl and marinate for at least 2 hours or refrigerate overnight. Scrape marinade from pork and reserve.

HEAT remaining 1/4 cup oil in a large skillet or sauté pan over high heat. Working in batches, add pork and sear on all sides, about 5 minutes. Remove pork from pan.

REDUCE heat to medium and add chorizo, onions, celery, red pepper, chili flakes and any reserved marinade. Cook, stirring, for 10 minutes, or until very soft and slightly browned.

ADD wine and tomatoes and bring to a boil. Reduce heat and simmer for 10 minutes, or until mixture is saucy.

INCREASE heat to medium-high and add clams. Cover and cook for 2 minutes. Return pork to pan, cover and cook for 1 to 2 minutes more, or until clams open and pork is hot. Discard any clams that haven't opened. Stir in remaining 1 tbsp coriander and 2 tbsp parsley.

Grilled Pork Chops in Adobo

SERVES 4

The secret to grilling pork chops is to grill on medium-low heat so the chops stay juicy instead of drying out. The adobo marinade, used extensively in Latin America, is a fragrant paste of garlic, herbs, cumin and sour citrus juice.

Serve the chops topped with tomato chutney.

1 tbsp chopped garlic	$\frac{1}{4}$ cup lime juice
1 tsp ground cumin	2 tbsp olive oil
1 tsp chopped fresh oregano, or $\frac{1}{4}$ tsp dried	4 rib or loin pork chops (about 1 inch thick)
1 tsp paprika	Salt and freshly ground pepper

COMBINE garlic, cumin, oregano, paprika, lime juice and oil in a bowl.

POUR marinade over pork chops and marinate for 1 hour at room temperature or 4 hours in refrigerator.

PREHEAT grill on medium-low. Season chops with salt and pepper.

GRILL chops for 4 minutes. Turn and grill for 4 minutes longer. Repeat, for a total grilling time of about 14 to 16 minutes, or until chops are just cooked.

{ tomato ginger chutney }

Heat 2 tbsp vegetable oil in a pot over medium heat. Add 1 thinly sliced small onion and sauté for 3 minutes, or until softened. Stir in 1 tbsp chopped garlic and 1 tbsp finely chopped gingerroot and cook for 30 seconds.

Add 6 seeded and diced canned or fresh tomatoes and cook for 5 minutes. Stir in 2 tbsp granulated sugar and 2 tbsp white vinegar and cook until mixture thickens, about 5 minutes.

Remove from heat and stir in 2 tbsp chopped fresh coriander and 2 tbsp lemon juice. Taste and adjust seasonings with salt and pepper. Cool.

Makes 1 $\frac{1}{2}$ cups.

Pork Spareribs

SERVES 4

In my opinion, the only way to cook pork spareribs is to precook the ribs in the oven and finish them on the grill. But you can also finish the ribs in the oven. Uncover them and continue to cook for 30 minutes (for crisper ribs, take the ribs out of the sauce for the final baking). I prefer pork back ribs, which are meatier and less fatty than side ribs, but side ribs are very flavourful. Both have their devotees.

Use homemade or storebought barbecue sauce.

1 tbsp chopped garlic	2 tbsp brown sugar
½ cup chopped onions	1 tsp hot pepper sauce
1 tbsp Dijon mustard	Salt to taste
½ cup beer	3 racks pork back ribs
1 cup barbecue sauce	

PREHEAT oven to 300 F.

COMBINE garlic, onions, mustard, beer, barbecue sauce, sugar, hot pepper sauce and salt in a pot. Bring to a boil over medium-high heat, then reduce heat and simmer for 10 minutes.

PLACE ribs in a baking dish and pour sauce over top. Cover dish tightly with foil and bake ribs for 1 ½ to 2 hours, or until fork-tender.

REMOVE ribs from baking dish. Skim fat from sauce and bring to a boil on medium heat and cook for about 3 to 5 minutes, or until thickened. Brush sauce over ribs.

PREHEAT grill on medium heat. Grill ribs for 20 minutes, basting and turning twice. Ribs should be glazed with sauce. Serve with reserved sauce on the side.

{ barbecue sauce }

Heat ¼ cup vegetable oil in a large skillet. Add 1 cup chopped onions, 2 tsp chopped garlic and 2 tsp chili flakes. Sauté for 2 minutes, or until onions soften. Stir in 3 cups pureed canned tomatoes, 2 tbsp cider vinegar, 2 tbsp brown sugar, 2 tbsp chili powder, 2 tsp ground cumin and salt to taste. Bring to a boil, reduce heat and simmer for 15 to 20 minutes, or until thickened.

Makes about 2 cups.

Cuban Stir-fry of Pork, Black Beans and Sweet Potatoes

SERVES 4

A tasty stir-fry. Use canned black beans and dice the sweet potato so it will cook quickly in the skillet. Serve over rice.

12 oz (375 g) pork tenderloin, cut in 1-inch cubes	1 14-oz (540 mL) can black beans, rinsed and drained
1 tsp ground cumin	$\frac{1}{4}$ cup orange juice
Salt and freshly ground pepper	$\frac{1}{4}$ cup lime juice
3 tbsp vegetable oil	$\frac{1}{2}$ cup chicken stock
1 tsp chopped garlic	$\frac{1}{4}$ tsp cayenne
1 sweet potato, peeled and diced	$\frac{1}{4}$ cup chopped fresh coriander
1 cup diced celery	

SEASON pork with cumin, salt and pepper.

HEAT a wok or large skillet over high heat. Add 2 tbsp oil and heat. Add pork and stir-fry for 3 minutes, or until browned on outside but still pink in centre. Remove from wok and reserve.

ADD remaining 1 tbsp oil and garlic to wok and stir-fry for 20 seconds. Add sweet potato and stir-fry for 2 minutes. Add celery and black beans. Stir together, cover and cook for 2 to 3 minutes, or until vegetables are tender-crisp.

RETURN meat and any juices to wok. Pour in orange juice, lime juice and stock and sprinkle with cayenne. Bring to a boil, then reduce heat and simmer for 1 minute. Sprinkle with coriander.

Pork and Leek Wellington with Port Sauce

SERVES 4

A sophisticated way to serve pork tenderloin. Enclosed in pastry, the meat cooks beautifully and stays moist. Serve with rapini or green beans. For a variation, use cranberry juice instead of pomegranate juice.

2 tbsp olive oil	**Port Sauce**
2 slices prosciutto, chopped	$\frac{1}{2}$ cup Port
3 leeks, white part only, chopped	$\frac{1}{2}$ cup pomegranate juice
1 tbsp Dijon mustard	1 cup chicken stock
$\frac{1}{4}$ cup whipping cream	1 tsp Dijon mustard
$\frac{1}{2}$ tsp dried thyme	$\frac{1}{4}$ cup whipping cream
6 oz (175 g) puff pastry, defrosted	
1 egg, beaten	
12 oz (375 g) pork tenderloin	
Salt and freshly ground pepper	

PREHEAT oven to 425 F.

HEAT oil in a skillet over medium heat. Add prosciutto and leeks and sauté for 3 minutes, or until softened. Stir in mustard, cream and thyme. Bring to a boil and cook until mixture is thick, about 1 minute.

ROLL puff pastry into a 12- by 10-inch rectangle. Spread leek mixture over pastry, leaving a 1-inch border on all sides. Brush borders with beaten egg.

PLACE pork on upper third of pastry along long side, tucking any thin ends of pork under. Season pork with salt and pepper. Fold short ends of pastry over ends of pork. Roll up pork in pastry until fully enclosed. Cut off excess pastry.

PLACE pastry seam side down on a baking sheet and cut 3 slashes across top. Brush with egg.

BAKE for 20 to 25 minutes, or until golden brown.

PREPARE sauce while pork is baking. Combine Port, pomegranate juice and stock in a pot. Bring to a boil and cook for 4 to 6 minutes, or until reduced to 1 cup. Stir in mustard and cream. Bring to a boil and cook for 2 minutes, or until slightly thickened.

CUT pork into slices and drizzle with sauce.

Roasted Veal Chops with Anchovy Aioli

SERVES 4

Veal is a boon to the person in a hurry because it needs little preparation and cooks quickly. Although the most tender cuts are expensive, there is very little fat or waste. Cook it until still slightly pink for the best flavour. Ask your butcher to clean the fat from the bones for you (ask for French-cut chops).

4 French-cut veal chops (12 oz/375 g each), about
    1¼ inches thick
2 tsp chopped fresh rosemary, or ½ tsp dried
1 tsp grated lemon rind
Salt and cracked black peppercorns
1 tbsp olive oil

Lemon Anchovy Aioli
¼ tsp chopped garlic
2 tsp chopped anchovy fillets
1 tbsp capers
½ cup mayonnaise
¼ tsp grated lemon rind
1 tsp lemon juice
2 tbsp whipping cream
Salt and freshly ground pepper

PREHEAT oven to 450 F.

SEASON chops with rosemary, lemon rind, salt and cracked pepper.

HEAT oil in an ovenproof skillet over medium-high heat. Sear chops for about 1 to 2 minutes per side, or until browned. Transfer skillet to oven and bake for 10 to 12 minutes, or until chops are just pink inside.

PREPARE aioli while chops are cooking by combining garlic, anchovies, capers, mayonnaise, lemon rind and lemon juice in a food processor or by hand. Stir in whipping cream and season with salt and pepper. Serve veal with a small dab of aioli and serve remaining aioli separately.

Roasted Veal Filet with Sage

SERVES 6

An easy but sophisticated dish with a wine-friendly sauce made with grapes. Garnish with little bunches of Champagne grapes.

2 tbsp Dijon mustard	Salt
2 tbsp chopped fresh sage	1 cup seedless red grapes, halved
1 tsp cracked black peppercorns	2 cups chicken stock
2 tbsp olive oil	1 tbsp balsamic vinegar
1 veal filet (about 2 lb/1 kg)	Fried sage leaves

PREHEAT oven to 400 F.

COMBINE mustard, sage, peppercorns and 1 tbsp oil. Spread over filet and season with a little salt.

HEAT remaining 1 tbsp oil in a large ovenproof skillet over medium-high heat. Brown veal for about 2 minutes per side.

TRANSFER skillet to oven and bake for 12 to 15 minutes, or until veal is still slightly pink inside.

REMOVE skillet from oven and transfer veal to a carving board.

DISCARD fat from skillet and add grapes, stock and vinegar. Bring to a boil, scraping up any little bits on bottom of skillet. Boil for 4 to 6 minutes, or until reduced by half.

STRAIN sauce, pressing down on grapes. Carve veal into ½-inch slices and serve with sauce and fried sage leaves.

{ frying herbs }

To fry sage or other fresh broad-leafed herbs, heat a little oil in a skillet over high heat. Add fresh sage leaves and sauté for about 30 seconds, or until crisp.

{ pastas, grains and legumes }

Penne with Spicy Marinara Sauce

SERVES 4

I love carbs, and pasta, rice and noodles are some of my favourite foods. I've learned that if you don't eat them, your brain is deprived of serotonin, the hormone you need to feel good. Now you know why so many people were miserable on those low-carb diets! Happily, the low-carb phase is a distant memory, and we are enjoying pasta once more.

A basic marinara sauce is a must for everyone's cooking repertoire. You can buy good prepared sauces, at a price, but it is very easy to make your own. This recipe yields twice as much sauce as you will need for four people, but it freezes well and is great to have on hand. Use it on pastas, as a sauce for grilled chicken, or as the base for a barbecue sauce.

The quality of the tomatoes is important. Ideally this should be made with fresh tomatoes (you'll need about 6 cups), but as good-quality fresh tomatoes are only available for about one month a year, I use canned. I try to buy San Marzano—the best Italian canned tomatoes—or organic.

This is a spicier sauce than a traditional marinara sauce. Omit or reduce the chili flakes if you wish.

2 28-oz (796 mL) cans tomatoes	6 fresh basil leaves, shredded
1/3 cup olive oil	1 tsp chili flakes, or more to taste
1 cup finely chopped onions	Salt and freshly ground pepper
2 tsp finely chopped garlic	1/2 cup grated Parmesan cheese
1 lb (500 g) penne	

CRUSH tomatoes with your hands or puree in a food processor along with their juices.

HEAT oil in a large sauté pan or skillet over medium-low heat. Add onions and sauté for about 5 minutes, or until softened. Add garlic and sauté for 1 minute.

ADD tomatoes with their juices. Increase heat and bring to a boil. Reduce heat and let sauce simmer for 45 to 60 minutes, or until thickened.

COOK pasta in a large pot of boiling salted water for about 10 minutes, or until *al dente*. Drain.

STIR basil, chili flakes, salt and pepper into sauce. Taste and adjust seasonings if necessary. Save half the sauce for another occasion. Combine remaining sauce with penne and toss with Parmesan.

In Italy most sauces call for dried pasta, and fresh is only used for the lighter, creamier sauces. It's a good rule, and I personally prefer good dried Italian pasta in most dishes. It has more flavour than the domestic variety and cooks to a real *al dente* stage.

The sauce dictates the pasta shape in recipes. As a rule of thumb, decide whether all the ingredients will stick to long pasta when it is twirled on a fork; otherwise use short pasta. The one exception to this is a seafood sauce, which is traditionally served with long pasta.

The shape of short pastas such as penne, fusilli and orecchiette helps them to catch pieces of chunkier sauces. Wider pastas such as fettuccine or tagliatelle are best for thicker, creamy sauces. Long thin pastas such as spaghettini or angelhair work best with lighter vegetable or seafood sauces that will not overwhelm the pasta and that contain bits that can be caught by the strands when they are twirled around a fork.

Tiny pastas such as orzo are used in soups or served as a side dish like rice.

ASIAN NOODLES • Chinese egg noodles come in different sizes. Some are broad, and some are thin like angelhair pasta; they are used in stir-fries, soups and salads. Most supermarkets carry a selection of both fresh and dried noodles, as do health food stores.

Wheat noodles, or somen, are white Japanese-style noodles made with wheat flour and water. Use them in soups or in salads, or substitute angelhair noodles.

Rice noodles are made with rice flour and water, sometimes with added cornstarch. They come in different sizes and only have to be soaked in hot water before cooking unless you deep-fry them. Use them in stir-fried dishes and soups. There is no substitute.

Soba noodles are Japanese buckwheat noodles—dark brown in colour and with a distinct buckwheat taste. Use them in soups and salads.

Udon noodles are white Japanese wheat noodles. They are quite thick and a bit chewy and have a distinctive, slippery texture. They are used in Japanese noodle soups.

Pasta with Goat Cheese and Mushrooms

SERVES 6 TO 8

Rigatoni or other tube-like pastas are excellent with this sauce, but you could also use fettuccine or tagliatelle. Freestyle baked pasta dishes like this one are less fussy and labour-intensive than lasagna. Use your favourite combination of fresh mushrooms; I like a mix of shiitake, oyster and brown (cremini) mushrooms.

1 oz (30 g) dried porcini mushrooms

1 lb (500 g) rigatoni

1/4 cup butter

1/4 cup all-purpose flour

2 cups milk

2 cups soft goat cheese

Salt and freshly ground pepper

3 tbsp olive oil

1 cup chopped onions

1 lb (500 g) mixed mushrooms, sliced

1 tsp chopped fresh thyme, or pinch dried

1 tbsp chopped garlic

1/4 cup chopped parsley

2 tbsp lemon juice

1 cup grated Parmesan cheese

SOAK dried mushrooms in 1 cup hot water for 20 minutes. Strain, reserving soaking liquid. Rinse mushrooms.

PREHEAT oven to 350 F.

COOK pasta in a large pot of boiling salted water for 10 minutes, or until *al dente*. Drain well and return to pot.

PREPARE sauce while pasta is cooking by heating butter in a pot over medium-high heat. Whisk in flour and cook for 1 minute. Pour in milk. Bring to a boil, whisking constantly to prevent lumps. Reduce heat and simmer for 5 minutes. Stir in goat cheese and season with salt and pepper.

HEAT oil in a skillet over medium-high heat. Add onions and sauté for 2 minutes, or until softened. Add fresh mushrooms and thyme and cook for about 2 minutes, or until mushrooms begin to release liquid.

ADD garlic, dried mushrooms and mushroom-soaking liquid to skillet. Bring to a boil and cook for 1 minute. Stir in parsley and lemon juice and season with salt and pepper.

STIR cheese sauce and mushrooms into noodles along with 1/2 cup Parmesan. Spoon into a large oiled baking dish and sprinkle with remaining 1/2 cup Parmesan. Bake for 25 minutes, or until heated through and browned.

Orecchiette with Prosciutto, Rapini and Beans

SERVES 4

The hot bean today is the Italian borlotti bean. They have always been popular in Italy but have finally hit the shores of our continent. If you can find them canned (or bottled), they are the best bean for this dish. If not, use Romano or cannellini beans.

1 bunch rapini, trimmed	2 oz (60 g) prosciutto, cut in 1-inch pieces
12 oz (375 g) orecchiette	1 ½ cups canned borlotti or other beans, rinsed
3 tbsp olive oil	and drained
1 tbsp chopped garlic	Salt and freshly ground pepper
½ tsp chili flakes	¼ cup grated Parmesan cheese

CUT rapini into 2-inch pieces, keeping stem pieces separate from tops.

BRING a large pot of salted water to a boil. Add rapini stems and cook for 1 minute. Add rapini tops and cook for 2 minutes longer, or until tender-crisp. Use a slotted spoon to remove rapini from water and rinse with cold water to stop cooking. Reserve.

ADD pasta to boiling water and cook for about 10 minutes, or until *al dente*. Drain, reserving ¼ cup cooking water.

HEAT oil in a large skillet over medium heat while pasta is cooking. Add garlic and sauté for 30 seconds, or until fragrant. Add chili flakes, reserved rapini, prosciutto and beans and sauté for 4 minutes, or until rapini and beans are warmed through.

TOSS hot pasta with rapini mixture and pasta cooking water. Season with salt and pepper. Drizzle with a little extra olive oil. Serve with Parmesan cheese on the side.

{ prosciutto }

Prosciutto is an air-cured ham that has firm, slightly salty meat surrounded by a thin ribbon of mellow fat. It ranges in colour from orangey pink to a deep red. It is wonderful eaten raw, accompanied by melon or figs. It also adds a concentrated flavour to a pasta sauce.

The finest prosciutto comes from the Parma region of Italy where, it is said, the quality of the air produces its superior flavour and texture.

Pasta Risotto with Clams

SERVES 4 AS AN APPETIZER; 2 AS A MAIN COURSE

This very tasty dish came about when *Harry Potter* cinematographer and New Zealand wine guru Michael Seresin took a long phone call while cooking pasta, leaving it to bubble away in a mixture of water and clam juice. He discovered that the pasta had absorbed all the flavour of the clam juice to create an incredible pasta dish.

In this recipe the pasta is cooked like risotto. Keep adding boiling water by the cup until the pasta is cooked.

¼ cup white wine	2 tsp chopped garlic
2 lb (1 kg) clams or mussels	4 tomatoes, seeded and chopped
2 cups fish stock or clam juice	Pinch chili flakes
1¼ cups water	2 tbsp shredded fresh basil
8 oz (250 g) spaghettini, broken in half	Salt and freshly ground pepper
2 tbsp olive oil	

BRING wine to a boil in a pot over high heat. Add clams, cover and steam until clams open, about 5 minutes. Drain clams, reserving liquid in a bowl. Discard any clams that haven't opened. Remove meat from clams and reserve in separate bowl. Leave a few clams in shells for garnish.

COMBINE reserved clam liquid, stock and water in a pot and bring to a simmer.

TRANSFER 2 cups simmering liquid to a non-stick sauté pan or large skillet and bring to a boil. Add spaghettini, reduce heat and simmer for 10 to 12 minutes, adding more hot stock as liquid boils away (add extra boiling water if you run out of stock).

HEAT oil in a separate skillet over medium heat while pasta is cooking. Add garlic and sauté for 30 seconds, or until garlic sizzles. Add tomatoes and chili flakes and cook for 5 minutes, or until tomatoes are softened.

ADD basil and reserved clam meat. Stir together and season well with salt and pepper. Cook until clams are hot, about 2 minutes. Toss sauce with spaghettini and any liquid in pan. Drizzle with a little extra olive oil, if desired.

Spaghetti with Meat Sauce

SERVES 4

This is my version of the classic meat sauce called Bolognese (a sauce that traditionally includes milk). Use it with spaghetti or as the basis for lasagna. It is a meat sauce, not a tomato sauce with meat. I use a mixture of veal and pork, but you could also use all veal.

This recipe makes about 8 cups sauce, which is too much for four people, so freeze half for another occasion.

2 28-oz (796 mL) cans tomatoes, drained	1 lb (500 g) ground veal
1/4 cup olive oil	1 lb (500 g) ground pork
2 oz (60 g) pancetta, chopped	Salt and freshly ground pepper
2 cups chopped onions	1/2 cup white wine
1/2 cup chopped carrots	2 cups beef stock
1/2 cup chopped celery	1/4 cup tomato paste
2 tsp chopped garlic	1 lb (500 g) spaghetti
1/4 cup chopped parsley	1/2 cup grated Parmesan cheese

CHOP or puree tomatoes and reserve.

HEAT oil in a sauté pan or large pot over medium-low heat. Add pancetta and sauté for 1 minute. Add onions, carrots and celery and cook gently for 10 minutes, or until vegetables are very soft and beginning to brown. Stir in garlic and parsley and cook for 3 minutes more.

INCREASE heat to medium. Add veal and pork, stirring to break up clumps of ground meat. Sauté until meat loses its pinkness, about 5 minutes. Season with salt and pepper.

ADD wine and boil until wine is mostly evaporated and mixture is saucy, about 4 minutes.

STIR in stock, tomato paste and reserved tomatoes. Bring to a boil, reduce heat, cover and simmer for 1 1/2 hours.

REMOVE lid, increase heat slightly and simmer for 15 to 30 minutes, or until sauce is thick and very tasty. Taste and reseason before serving.

COOK spaghetti in a large pot of boiling salted water for 8 minutes, or until *al dente*. Drain well and serve with sauce and cheese (save leftover sauce for another time).

Tagliatelle with Scallops, Lemon and Breadcrumbs

SERVES 4

This terrific dish is simple to make and complex in flavour. You can prepare the sauce and breadcrumbs ahead of time and boil the pasta just before you need it. Breadcrumbs were once considered the poor man's Parmesan.

12 oz tagliatelle

1/4 cup olive oil

1 tbsp chopped garlic

1/2 cup fresh breadcrumbs

2 tbsp chopped parsley

1 leek, white and light-green part only, sliced

12 oz scallops, cut in 1/2-inch dice

1 tsp grated lemon rind

3 tbsp lemon juice

Salt and freshly ground pepper

COOK pasta in a large pot of boiling salted water for 10 minutes, or until *al dente*. Drain pasta, reserving 1/4 cup pasta cooking water.

PREPARE sauce while pasta is cooking by heating 1 tbsp olive oil in a small skillet over medium heat. Add 1 tsp garlic and breadcrumbs. Sauté for about 2 minutes, or until breadcrumbs are crisp. Stir in 1 tbsp parsley. Reserve.

HEAT remaining 3 tbsp oil in a large skillet over medium-high heat. Add leeks and sauté for 1 minute. Add scallops and remaining 2 tsp garlic and sauté for 1 minute. Stir in lemon rind and 2 tbsp lemon juice. Season well with salt and pepper.

TOSS drained pasta with scallops. Stir in reserved pasta cooking water, remaining 1 tbsp lemon juice and remaining 1 tbsp parsley. Serve sprinkled with breadcrumbs. Drizzle with a little extra olive oil.

Shrimp and Soba Noodle Stir-fry

SERVES 2 AS A MAIN COURSE; 4 AS AN APPETIZER

The combination of tastes, textures and visual appeal make this a great dish for entertaining. Baby bok choy, a Chinese cabbage, is sold in a tiny form (the size of a baby's hand) in Asian and some regular supermarkets. If you can only buy the larger version, slice each one (you'll need about 2 cups) or use baby spinach.

For a stunning presentation, finish the dish without adding the bok choy. Pile the noodles on a platter, surround with the bok choy and drizzle with a little sauce from the wok.

Spicy Wasabi Sauce

2 tbsp sesame oil

2 tsp wasabi paste

3 tbsp soy sauce

3 tbsp rice vinegar

3 tbsp mirin

2 tbsp chopped pickled ginger

Noodles

16 small baby bok choy

8 oz (250 g) soba noodles

2 tbsp vegetable oil

1 tsp chopped garlic

2 tbsp chopped gingerroot

1/4 cup chopped shallots or red onions

8 oz (250 g) large shrimp, peeled

1 cup slivered green onions

Salt and freshly ground pepper

2 tbsp toasted sesame seeds

WHISK sesame oil, wasabi, soy sauce, vinegar, mirin and pickled ginger in a bowl. Reserve.

BRING a large pot of salted water to a boil. Add bok choy and cook for 1 minute. Remove bok choy with a slotted spoon, refresh with cold water until cool and drain well. Reserve.

ADD noodles to pot and boil until *al dente*, about 3 to 4 minutes. Drain and reserve.

HEAT a large wok or skillet over high heat while noodles are cooking. Add oil and heat. Add garlic, gingerroot and shallots. Stir-fry for 1 minute. Stir in shrimp and stir-fry for 2 minutes, or until pink.

ADD green onions and reserved sauce to skillet. Bring to a boil. Add reserved noodles and bok choy. Toss everything together and cook, stirring occasionally, until noodles are hot. Adjust seasonings, adding soy sauce or salt and pepper if needed. Garnish with sesame seeds.

Shanghai Noodles with Black Beans

SERVES 2 AS A MAIN COURSE; 4 IF SERVED WITH OTHER DISHES

This traditional noodle dish is perfect for a weekday family dinner because it's quick to make and a favourite with kids. Buy bottled black bean sauce at the supermarket. Substitute chicken or shrimp for the pork.

8 oz (250 g) fresh Chinese noodles
8 oz (250 g) boneless pork
Salt and freshly ground pepper
1 tbsp vegetable oil
2 tsp chopped garlic
2 tsp chopped gingerroot
1 small red onion, cut in ¼-inch slices
½ red pepper, cut in ¼-inch strips

2 tbsp black bean sauce
2 tbsp soy sauce
1 tsp hot Asian chili sauce
1 tsp granulated sugar
1 cup chicken stock
1 tbsp rice vinegar
1 tsp sesame oil

COOK noodles in a large pot of boiling salted water for 2 minutes, or until tender. Refresh with cold water, drain and reserve.

CUT pork into strips about 2 inches long and ½ inch wide. Season with salt and pepper.

HEAT a wok or large skillet over high heat. Add vegetable oil and heat. Add garlic and ginger and stir-fry for 30 seconds. Add pork and stir-fry until it is just pink, about 2 minutes. Remove pork from wok with a slotted spoon and reserve.

ADD onion and red pepper to wok. Stir-fry for about 2 minutes, or until vegetables are slightly softened.

STIR in black bean sauce, soy sauce, chili sauce, sugar, stock and vinegar. Bring to a boil.

ADD pork, noodles and sesame oil to wok and toss together. Cook over medium heat for 30 seconds, or until pork and noodles are hot and coated with sauce.

Mussels with Thai Noodles

SERVES 4 TO 6

This is a store-cupboard dish if you use the large, tasty, green-lipped New Zealand mussels. You buy them precooked and frozen on the half shell, and they are best added to a dish in the frozen state. If you use fresh mussels, steam them in the coconut milk sauce until they open.

8 oz (250 g) linguine-sized rice noodles

2 tbsp vegetable oil

½ cup chopped red onions

1 tsp chopped garlic

1 14-oz (400 mL) can coconut milk

2 tbsp fish sauce

1 tsp grated lime rind

1 tbsp lime juice

1 tsp hot Asian chili sauce

1 tsp granulated sugar

2 lb (1 kg) frozen green-lipped New Zealand mussels

2 tbsp chopped fresh mint or coriander

2 tbsp chopped fresh Thai or regular basil

SOAK noodles in hot water for 20 minutes. Drain well.

PREPARE sauce while noodles are soaking by heating oil in a large pot or wok over medium heat. Add onions and garlic and sauté until golden at edges, about 2 minutes.

STIR in coconut milk, fish sauce, lime rind and juice, chili sauce and sugar. Bring to a boil and cook for 2 minutes to amalgamate flavours. Reduce heat to medium-low.

ADD mussels. Cover and steam until mussels are heated through, about 4 minutes.

STIR in mint, basil and drained noodles. Simmer for 1 to 2 minutes, or until noodles are softened and hot.

Basmati Rice Pilau

SERVES 4

A quick, foolproof way to cook slender, nutty basmati rice. An excellent side dish for all things Indian.

2 cups basmati rice	2 bay leaves
2 cups water	2 1-inch cinnamon sticks
1 tsp ground turmeric	1 cup green peas
1 tsp cumin seeds	Salt to taste
6 whole cloves	

SOAK rice in cold water for 30 minutes. Drain.

COMBINE rice, water, turmeric, cumin, cloves, bay leaves and cinnamon in a heavy pot. Bring to a boil over high heat. Cover, reduce heat to low and cook for 12 to 15 minutes, or until rice is tender.

REMOVE from heat and stir in peas and salt. Cover and let sit for 5 minutes. Remove bay leaves and cinnamon sticks before serving.

{ turmeric }

Turmeric is a root that adds a bright yellow colour to dishes. It is traditionally used in Indian dishes but has become a trendy spice in other cuisines as well. Handle it carefully, because it can stain clothes if spilled.

Risotto

SERVES 4 AS AN APPETIZER; 2 AS A MAIN COURSE

This is the traditional risotto recipe. Served with a salad, it makes a quick and easy meal if you are in a hurry and have all the ingredients on hand.

5 cups chicken stock	1½ cups Carnaroli or arborio rice
2 tbsp olive oil	¼ cup grated Parmesan cheese
2 tbsp butter	2 tbsp chopped parsley
½ cup finely chopped onions	Salt and freshly ground pepper

HEAT stock in a pot until simmering.

HEAT oil and 1 tbsp butter in a large, heavy pot over medium heat. Add onions and sauté for 2 minutes. Add rice and sauté until grains are coated with oil, about 1 minute.

POUR in 1 cup hot stock and cook, stirring, until most of stock is absorbed. Continue to add stock in 1-cup quantities, stirring most of the time, until rice is creamy with a slight bite in centre, about 20 to 25 minutes.

REMOVE from heat and stir in remaining 1 tbsp butter, cheese and parsley. Season well with salt and pepper. Serve immediately.

{ making risotto }

Risotto's creamy texture can only be obtained when you use a rice that

has the starch to bind the kernels together and at the same time leave the rice *al dente* (with a bit of firmness) when cooked. Carnaroli is the rice of choice for the best risotto. More expensive and less available than arborio, it is worth seeking out. It has lots of soft starch for the creamy consistency but retains a good firm bite when cooked. Stir the risotto regularly to release the starch. It takes about 20 minutes from start to finish. Use a heavy pot to retain heat and keep the risotto cooking evenly without scorching.

Good stock is essential in risotto because the rice absorbs the flavour (though at a fine restaurant in Italy I once saw a chef add a bouillon cube to risotto near the end of the cooking time!). Traditionally the stock is added to the rice just a ½ cup at a time, but as a lazy cook, I add it a cup at a time, and don't notice much difference.

Risotto with Scallops and Roasted Cauliflower

SERVES 4 AS AN APPETIZER

This dish is a perfect combination of tastes and textures; it is one of the most popular recipes I've developed for the *Globe and Mail*. The little muscle that attaches the scallop to its shell should be removed before cooking.

Roasted Cauliflower

2 cups cauliflower florets (cut in bite-sized pieces)

1 tbsp olive oil

Salt and freshly ground pepper

Scallops

1 tbsp olive oil

12 large scallops

Salt and freshly ground pepper

Risotto

3 tbsp butter

$\frac{1}{2}$ cup finely chopped onions

$\frac{1}{2}$ tsp finely chopped garlic

1 cup Carnaroli or arborio rice

$\frac{1}{2}$ cup white wine

4 cups hot chicken stock

$\frac{1}{4}$ cup grated Parmesan cheese

2 tbsp chopped parsley

Salt and freshly ground pepper

PREHEAT oven to 425 F.

TOSS cauliflower, oil, salt and pepper in a large bowl. Spread on a baking sheet and roast, stirring occasionally, for 15 minutes, or until golden and tender. Reserve.

HEAT 2 tbsp butter in a heavy pot over medium heat for risotto. Add onions and garlic and sauté for 2 minutes. Add rice and stir to coat with butter, about 1 minute. Pour in wine and simmer until wine is nearly absorbed.

ADD 1 cup hot stock and simmer until stock is nearly absorbed. Continue adding stock a cup at a time until 3 cups stock have been absorbed (about 20 minutes in total). Stir in reserved cauliflower. Add remaining stock and cook until rice is *al dente*.

PREPARE scallops by heating oil in a skillet over high heat while risotto is cooking. Season scallops with salt and pepper and fry for 2 minutes per side, or until golden.

STIR in remaining 1 tbsp butter, cheese and parsley. Season with salt and pepper. Serve risotto in soup bowls topped with scallops.

Rice is the staple food for almost half the world's population. (In the Chinese and Thai languages, the word for rice and food is the same.) It is grown in Asia, Africa, the Mediterranean countries, the U.S. and South America, and it varies in size, taste and texture depending on where it is grown.

- Japanese rice is a semi-glutinous short-grain rice. The rice grains are short and quite glossy and, when cooked, the rice is slightly sticky. Rinse it before cooking to remove some of the surface starch. Japanese rice can be used as a substitute for sticky rice in Asian recipes. It is also good in rice stuffings, when you don't want dry, fluffy grains.

- Thai jasmine is a long-grain rice used in Asian dishes. It has long, slender grains and a subtle perfumed scent. It is moist and tender but not fluffy. Rinse it before using to remove the surface starch.

- Basmati is long-grain Indian rice with a slightly nutty flavour. Rinse and soak it before using. It requires less water for cooking than other long-grain rice.

- Sticky (glutinous) rice can be either long-grain or short-grain. The porcelain-coloured grains must be soaked for several hours if the rice is steamed, but can be quick-soaked for 15 minutes before being boiled. The sticky texture is good for dim sum or in stuffings, but I also love it as a side dish with stir-fried shiitake or Chinese mushrooms.

- Italian arborio rice has large, plump grains and a slightly nutty taste. Because of its somewhat sticky texture, it makes excellent puddings and good risotto. However, the best rice for risotto is Carnaroli, which has an even creamier texture than arborio, while still retaining some bite when cooked.

Grain Pilaf

SERVES 4

I make this whenever I have a craving for healthy food. Grains are enjoying a renaissance, as they help keep blood sugars down, lower cholesterol and, as complex carbohydrates, they are fat free and easy to burn. Used in a pilaf like this one, they taste pretty good, too. The lentils add colour, texture and protein. Serve as a vegetarian main course with a salad, or as a side dish with chicken or fish.

½ cup lentils du Puy	¼ cup quinoa, rinsed
2 ½ cups water	Salt and freshly ground pepper
½ cup bulgur	2 tbsp chopped parsley

COMBINE lentils and water in a large pot and bring to a boil. Reduce heat, cover and simmer for 20 minutes.

ADD bulgur and quinoa, cover and simmer for 15 minutes longer, or until grains are cooked. Drain off any excess water. Season with salt and pepper and garnish with parsley.

{ quinoa }

Quinoa (pronounced KEENwah) is high in protein and iron and is an essential part of a good vegetarian diet. It has a slightly sweet, earthy taste and is excellent in mixed-grain dishes. Always rinse it before using.

{ bulgur }

Bulgur is the Turkish name for cracked wheat berries. Its nutty flavour and ease of preparation (it can just be soaked in hot water before eating) make it a handy staple to have on hand. It is excellent in salads (such as tabbouleh) or mixed with other grains.

Kasha and Wild Mushroom Gratin

SERVES 4

Kasha is toasted buckwheat. Buckwheat is a typical grain in Eastern Europe, where it is served as a side dish with meat or poultry or mixed with short noodles as a vegetarian main course. Buy it at the supermarket. Adding egg brings out the toasty flavour and helps to separate the grains.

²/₃ cup butter	3 tbsp chopped fresh dill
2 cups chopped onions	Salt and freshly ground pepper
10 oz (300 g) mixed mushrooms, including shiitake (stemmed), oyster and brown, sliced	1 cup kasha
	1 egg, beaten
½ cup sour cream	2 cups chicken stock or water

HEAT ¼ cup butter in a large ovenproof skillet over medium heat. Add onions and sauté until tinged with brown, about 5 to 6 minutes. Stir in mushrooms and sauté for 3 minutes longer, or until mushrooms release their liquid.

ADD sour cream and dill and cook for 1 minute, but do not allow to boil. Season well with salt and pepper.

PREHEAT oven to 325 F.

COMBINE kasha and egg in a bowl. Add to a non-stick skillet over medium heat and stir until kasha is dry, about 3 minutes. Add stock and bring to a boil. Reduce heat and simmer, covered, for 10 minutes, or until all liquid is absorbed.

STIR kasha into mushroom mixture. Taste and adjust seasonings if necessary. Dot kasha and mushrooms with remaining butter and bake for 15 to 20 minutes, or until heated through.

Barley and Squash Risotto

SERVES 4

Barley makes an excellent, nutty risotto because it can be cooked to a creamy consistency. Adapt your favourite risotto recipe to barley using this method. The most important thing to remember is to stir for the last 10 minutes of cooking so the mixture will be creamy.

5 cups chicken stock or water	1 cup pearl barley
2 tbsp olive oil	Salt and freshly ground pepper to taste
1/2 cup finely chopped onions	1/2 cup grated Parmesan cheese
1 tsp chopped garlic	2 tbsp chopped parsley
2 cups diced butternut or pepper squash	

HEAT stock in a pot over medium heat until simmering.

HEAT oil in a heavy pot over medium heat. Add onions and sauté for 1 minute. Add garlic and sauté for 1 minute longer, or until onions are softened.

STIR in squash and sauté for 2 minutes. Stir in barley and sauté for 1 minute, or until barley is coated with oil.

ADD 1 cup hot stock, bring to a boil and simmer, stirring occasionally, until barley absorbs most of stock. Add 2 more cups stock, cover and cook for 20 minutes, or until most of stock has been absorbed.

STIR in 1 cup additional stock and cook, uncovered, stirring frequently, until stock has been absorbed, about 5 minutes. Add remaining stock and cook, stirring, until barley is tender, about 10 minutes longer. Season well with salt and pepper.

STIR in parsley and cheese and serve immediately. (Risotto thickens as it sits, but you can beat in more stock or water if you reheat it.)

{ barley }

Barley is sold as pot or pearl barley. Pearl barley is more refined than pot; it has been polished longer and the grains are smaller. It takes less time to cook but is slightly less nutritious.

Pepper and Broccoli Couscous

SERVES 4

Serve this as a side dish with pork, lamb or poultry. It can also be served as a vegetarian main course with a chickpea salad (page 74).

Instead of broccoli, you can use broccolini, cauliflower or edamame.

2 tbsp olive oil	2 cups couscous
1 cup diced broccoli florets	2 cups chicken stock or water
1 cup diced red peppers	3 green onions, chopped
1 tsp ground cumin	1/2 cup toasted pine nuts
1/2 tsp paprika	Salt and freshly ground pepper
1 cup green peas	

HEAT oil in a large skillet over medium heat. Add broccoli and peppers. Sauté for 2 to 3 minutes, or until softened.

STIR in cumin and paprika, reduce heat to medium-low and continue to cook for 5 minutes, or until vegetables are tender and peppers are slightly blackened. Stir in peas. Reserve.

PLACE couscous in a large bowl. Bring stock to a boil in a pot. Pour stock over couscous, stir and cover. Let stand for 5 minutes.

STIR in vegetables, green onions and pine nuts. Cover and let stand for 2 more minutes. Season with salt and pepper.

{ couscous }

COUSCOUS is a grain-sized pasta indigenous to North Africa. It is made with semolina that has been cooked and then broken up into tiny grains by sieving. It is used in Moroccan and Algerian cooking and can be served as a side dish or incorporated into a main dish.

Israeli Couscous with Feta

SERVES 4

A deliciously rich dish to serve with chicken and fish and anything with a Mediterranean flavour.

2 cups Israeli couscous	Salt and freshly ground pepper
1/2 cup feta cheese	2 tbsp chopped fresh dill or parsley
1/2 cup whipping cream	

BRING a large pot of water to a boil. Add Israeli couscous and boil for 7 to 9 minutes, or until tender. Drain well and return to pot.

STIR in feta and cream and cook gently just until feta melts. Season with salt and pepper and garnish with dill.

{ israeli couscous }

Israeli couscous is also known as pearl pasta or pearl couscous. It is round and larger than regular couscous. It is served as a side dish, in salads and in soups.

Spiced Lentil Mash

SERVES 4

One of my favourite dishes, you can serve this as a side dish with almost any kind of meal. Use red lentils, as they fall to a puree when cooked.

2 tbsp butter	4 cups chicken stock or water
$\frac{1}{2}$ cup chopped onions	Salt
1 tbsp Indian curry paste	2 tbsp chopped fresh coriander
1 $\frac{1}{2}$ cups red lentils	

HEAT butter in a pot over medium heat. Add onions and sauté for 4 minutes, or until beginning to brown on edges. Stir in curry paste and cook for 1 minute.

STIR in lentils and coat with curry paste. Pour in stock and bring to a boil. Reduce heat and simmer for 18 to 20 minutes, or until lentils fall to a puree. Season well with salt and stir in coriander.

{ lentils }

Red lentils are split and have no outer husk. They cook to a porridge-like consistency. Green or brown lentils retain their outer husks and hold their shape when cooked. They are good in salads. Lentils from Le Puy in France are small green lentils that have more flavour and texture than other green or brown lentils, though they also take a little longer to cook.

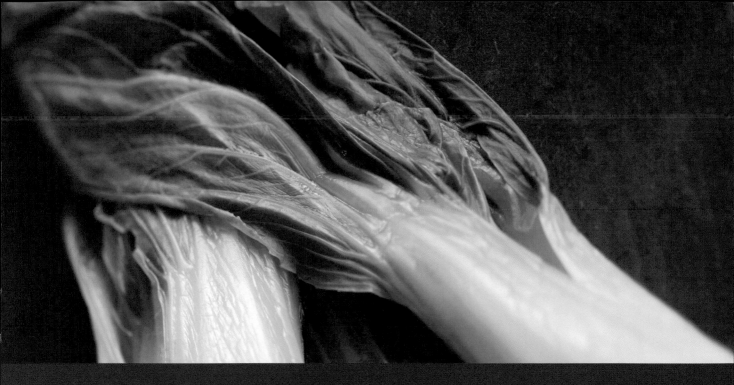

{ vegetables }

Potato Gratin with Onions and Goat Cheese

SERVES 8 TO 10

For me, a meal is not complete without a potato of some kind. This fancy potato gratin is wonderful with chicken and lamb. The goat cheese is just a whisper in the background.

Gratin refers to the shallow dish that these potatoes are baked in; contrary to popular opinion, gratins do not necessarily include cheese (although this one does).

¼ cup butter

2 large onions, thinly sliced

Salt

1 cup soft goat cheese

1 ½ cups milk

1 cup whipping cream

3 lb (1.5 kg) Yukon Gold potatoes, peeled and thinly sliced

¼ cup chopped mixed fresh herbs such as parsley, sage, chives or rosemary

Freshly ground pepper

PREHEAT oven to 400 F.

HEAT 2 tbsp butter in a large skillet over medium heat. Add onions, sprinkle with salt and sauté, stirring occasionally, until onions are soft and caramelized, about 10 to 12 minutes.

COMBINE goat cheese, milk and cream in a pot over low heat, stirring until goat cheese is incorporated.

ARRANGE one-third of potatoes over bottom of a large buttered gratin dish. Layer half the onions and half the herbs on top and season with salt and pepper. Repeat layers, finishing with a layer of potatoes.

POUR hot goat cheese mixture over potatoes. The liquid should barely cover potatoes. Add more milk if needed.

DOT with remaining 2 tbsp butter and bake for 50 to 60 minutes, or until potatoes are cooked through and top is browned.

{ potatoes }

Yukon Gold potatoes are good for all types of mashed, baked and roasted
potato dishes. If you can't find them, use any baking potatoes.

I use red-skinned waxy potatoes, which have less starch, in salads, and in boiled and steamed dishes, but they are also good for roasting and they add an unusual texture to mashes.

Fingerling potatoes look like little fat fingers. They are great roasted, steamed or boiled.

Smashed Creamers with Garlic Chips

SERVES 4 TO 6

Creamers are red-skinned potatoes, and they give this mashed potato dish a slightly lumpy texture that is perfect with grilled dishes. The garlic becomes sweet when cooked and adds crunch to the potatoes.

2 lb (1 kg) red potatoes, peeled and cut in even-sized chunks
Salt and freshly ground pepper

½ cup butter
4 large garlic cloves, thinly sliced

COVER potatoes with cold salted water in a pot and bring to a boil. Simmer for 10 to 15 minutes, or until potatoes are tender. Drain potatoes well, leave in pot and shake pot, uncovered, over turned-off burner or very low heat to dry out potatoes.

SEASON potatoes with salt and pepper and mash with a fork, leaving lots of texture in potatoes.

MELT butter in a small skillet over low heat while potatoes are cooking. Add garlic and sauté for about 5 to 7 minutes, or until golden.

STRAIN butter over potatoes, reserving garlic chips, and gently combine with potatoes. Season again if needed. Serve potatoes scattered with reserved garlic.

{ draining potatoes }

To make sure boiled potatoes are nice and dry for mashing or roasting, I drain them, return them to the hot pot, and then shake the pot, uncovered, over the turned-off or low-heat burner to dry them out. This also roughens up the outsides a bit, and the potatoes crisp more easily when they are roasted.

Make-ahead Mashed Potatoes

A good dish for a crowd or buffet. It will keep for two days in the refrigerator before baking and can even be frozen. Bake directly from the frozen state for 1 hour, or until heated through.

4 lb (2 kg) Yukon Gold potatoes, peeled and
    quartered
½ cup butter, cubed
2 eggs, beaten

½ cup milk
Pinch ground nutmeg
Salt and freshly ground pepper

PLACE potatoes in a pot and cover with cold salted water. Bring to a boil and boil for 10 to 15 minutes, or until potatoes are tender. Drain potatoes in pot. Place uncovered pot back over turned-off burner or very low heat and shake pot to dry potatoes.

MASH potatoes. Beat in butter, eggs and enough milk to produce the consistency you want. Season with nutmeg, salt and pepper.

SPOON potatoes into a large buttered gratin dish. Cover and refrigerate until needed.

PREHEAT oven to 350 F.

BAKE potatoes for 20 to 30 minutes, or until heated through.

Garlicky Potato Puree

SERVES 6

This puree is very soft and rich, and it goes very well with beef dishes. You can cut the calories by replacing the whipping cream with light sour cream or even the potato cooking water, but it will not taste as heavenly.

Buy roasted garlic puree or roast your own.

2 lb (1 kg) Yukon Gold potatoes, peeled and
    quartered
3 tbsp roasted garlic puree
$\frac{1}{2}$ cup whipping cream

2 tbsp butter
$\frac{1}{2}$ to 1 cup beef stock
Salt and freshly ground pepper

PLACE potatoes in a pot and cover with cold salted water. Bring to a boil and boil for 10 to 15 minutes, or until tender. Drain potatoes in pot and shake pot over turned-off burner or very low heat to dry out potatoes.

PUREE potatoes with an electric mixer or by hand, slowly beating in garlic, cream, butter and stock. Potatoes should be very soft and fluffy. Season with salt and pepper.

{ roasting garlic }

When roasted, whole garlic turns into a mild-mannered vegetable. It becomes soft and mellow and loses its characteristic bite. Combine it with goat cheese for a spread, add it to sauces, or beat it into mashed potatoes. It will keep for about a week in the refrigerator.

Cut off the top third of the garlic head to expose the cloves. Rub the exposed cloves with oil. Wrap in foil and bake at 400 F for 45 to 60 minutes, or until garlic is soft and slightly brown.

Squeeze garlic out of skins into a bowl and discard skins. One head of garlic yields about 3 tbsp puree.

Spiced Mashed Potatoes with Coconut Milk

SERVES 6

A fabulous spicy mashed potato. Serve it with Indian roast chicken or other Asian-inspired dishes.

2 lb (1 kg) Yukon Gold potatoes, peeled and cut in even-sized chunks

1 tbsp Thai red curry paste

1 cup coconut milk

Salt and freshly ground pepper

2 tbsp chopped fresh coriander

PLACE potatoes in a pot and cover with cold salted water. Stir in curry paste. Bring to a boil and boil for 10 to 15 minutes, or until potatoes are tender. Drain, reserving about ½ cup cooking liquid. Shake pot with drained potatoes, uncovered, over turned-off burner or very low heat to dry potatoes.

BRING coconut milk to a boil in a small pot while potatoes are cooking. Boil for about 8 minutes, or until reduced to ½ cup.

MASH potatoes and beat in coconut milk and about ¼ cup cooking liquid. Season with salt and pepper. For a spicier mash, beat in more reserved potato water. Sprinkle with coriander.

Sautéed Potatoes with Ham and Cheese

SERVES 4

This incredible potato dish is so good that I often eat it on its own for a quick meal with a salad, but you could also serve it with plain grilled meat, chicken or an omelette. Omit the prosciutto if desired.

3 cups diced red potatoes	4 slices prosciutto, cut in strips
2 cups chicken stock	2 leeks, trimmed and cut in $1/2$-inch slices
1 tbsp olive oil	4 oz (125 g) Fontina cheese, diced

COMBINE potatoes and stock in a large non-stick skillet. Bring to a boil and cook, uncovered, until potatoes are tender-crisp and stock has just about disappeared, about 5 to 8 minutes. Drain potatoes and reserve. Wipe out skillet.

ADD oil to skillet and heat over medium heat. Add prosciutto and leeks and sauté for 2 minutes, or until leeks are limp. Add potatoes and sauté for about 5 minutes, or until potatoes are tender and golden.

REDUCE heat to low, add cheese and cover. Cook for 3 minutes, or until cheese melts.

{ leeks }

As leeks grow, soil is mounded up around the base to keep them white (only the green leaves appear above the ground), but this also means that earth becomes embedded between the layers. To clean leeks, cut off the roots and the dark-green tops (discard or freeze to use in stocks). Cut down through the centre of the leek to expose the layers, open up the leek and rinse under warm water (warm water will dislodge the soil more effectively than cold water).

Grilled Red Potatoes with Greek Herbs

SERVES 4

This wonderfully tasty dish is perfect with roast chicken. It also tastes great at room temperature. If you prefer not to grill, bake the potatoes in a covered pan at 450 F for 20 minutes.

1 ½ lb (750 g) small red potatoes, halved
¼ cup olive oil
Salt and freshly ground pepper
¼ cup chopped green onions
1 tbsp chopped fresh oregano

1 tbsp chopped parsley
2 tsp finely chopped garlic
¼ tsp grated lemon rind
3 tbsp lemon juice

TOSS potatoes in a grill-proof pan (preferably metal) with 2 tbsp oil, salt and pepper. Cover with foil.

PREHEAT grill on high.

PLACE pan on grill, close lid and cook for 20 minutes, or until potatoes are brown and tender, shaking pan occasionally.

COMBINE green onions, oregano, parsley, garlic, lemon rind, lemon juice and remaining 2 tbsp oil in a bowl. Toss with warm potatoes. Taste and adjust seasonings if necessary.

Old-fashioned Roasted Potatoes

SERVES 6 TO 8

The Scottish way to roast potatoes is to partially cook them first. Crisp and golden on the outside, meltingly soft inside, these potatoes are perfect with turkey, roast beef or lamb. In Scotland my mother would cook them in beef or duck fat, and it's still the best taste in the world.

3 lb (1.5 kg) Yukon Gold potatoes, peeled and cut in even-sized chunks	¼ cup olive oil or other fat Salt and freshly ground pepper

PREHEAT oven to 400 F.

PLACE potatoes in a pot and cover with cold salted water. Bring to a boil and cook for 7 minutes. Drain and place pot back on turned-off burner. Shake pot to roughen surface of potatoes (this gives them crunchy edges).

TOSS potatoes with fat and season with salt and pepper. Arrange in a metal roasting pan in a single layer. Roast, turning occasionally, for 45 to 60 minutes, or until golden brown and cooked through.

{ roasting vegetables }

Root vegetables are sensational when roasted. Roasted potatoes, turnips, parsnips, sweet potatoes, Jerusalem artichokes and carrots have crisp outer skins and sweet, mellow centres. They go particularly well with roast meats. Roast some unpeeled garlic cloves alongside them for added flavour, then squeeze the creamy cloves out of the skins and serve them with the vegetables.

To prepare vegetables for roasting, cut them into even-sized pieces. Size and shape does not matter as long as they are all similar. Potatoes, turnips, parsnips, whole onions and carrots benefit from blanching (brief boiling) before roasting. Place in a pot of cold salted water, bring to a boil and boil for 5 to 7 minutes. Drain well.

Sweet potatoes, fennel or green vegetables such as Brussels sprouts do not need to be blanched before roasting.

Root Vegetable Gratin

SERVES 4 AS A MAIN COURSE; 6 TO 8 AS A SIDE DISH

This is a terrific and very tasty vegetarian main course or a delicious side dish to go with chicken or meat. You can change the variety of vegetables, depending on your own favourites.

1 small rutabaga	1 tsp dried thyme
3 Yukon Gold potatoes	Salt and freshly ground pepper
3 carrots	¾ cup milk
3 parsnips	¾ cup whipping cream
3 tbsp butter	1 cup grated mozzarella or Cheddar cheese
1 ½ cups chopped leeks (white part only)	1 cup grated pecorino or Parmesan cheese
2 tbsp chopped garlic	

PREHEAT oven to 400 F.

PEEL rutabaga, potatoes, carrots and parsnips and cut into ¾-inch chunks. Place rutabaga in a large pot of salted water and bring to a boil.

ADD potatoes, carrots and parsnips. Cook for 5 minutes, or until all vegetables are tender-crisp but still have some texture. Drain vegetables and return to pot. Place pot over turned-off burner and stir vegetables to evaporate any remaining water.

MELT 2 tbsp butter in a skillet over medium heat. Add leeks and sauté for 2 minutes, or until softened. Add garlic and thyme and cook for 1 minute. Add to root vegetable mixture and season well with salt and pepper.

COMBINE milk and cream in a pot and bring just to a boil (or microwave).

SPREAD half the vegetable mixture in a shallow baking dish. Sprinkle with half the mozzarella and half the pecorino. Spread remaining vegetables over cheese and pour hot cream/milk mixture over top. Sprinkle with remaining cheeses and dot with remaining 1 tbsp butter.

BAKE for 35 to 40 minutes, or until vegetables are soft and have absorbed almost all liquid.

Sauté of Garlic Scapes and Green Beans

SERVES 6

The beans and the scapes look remarkably similar, making this dish a bit of a taste surprise. Serve it with any sautéed or grilled poultry or meat. If scapes are unavailable, just use more beans. Blanch the vegetables ahead of time and sauté just before serving.

8 oz (250 g) green beans, trimmed	½ red pepper, thinly sliced
6 oz (175 g) garlic scapes, trimmed	1 tbsp balsamic vinegar
1 tbsp olive oil	Salt and freshly ground pepper

BRING a large pot of salted water to a boil. Add beans and cook for 3 minutes.

CUT scapes same length as beans. Add to beans and blanch for 1 to 2 minutes, or until vegetables are tender-crisp. Drain beans and scapes and refresh with cold water.

HEAT oil in a large skillet over medium heat. Add red pepper and sauté for 2 minutes. Add beans and scapes, toss together, cover skillet and cook for 2 minutes.

SEASON with vinegar, salt and pepper.

{ garlic scapes }

Garlic scapes

Garlic scapes are a hot new vegetable in the market, although they have been around since garlic was first grown. Scapes are the edible curly tops and seed pods of hard-necked garlic. The scapes form in early summer and are cut off in June or July to allow the garlic bulbs to grow larger. The taste of scapes is much milder than garlic. Mediterranean countries use them extensively as a vegetable or seasoning. At present, they are only available fresh in specialty food stores or farmers' markets. Trim them by removing any large seed pods.

Sautéed garlic scapes are similar to a garlicky green bean and are an excellent accompaniment for meat or chicken. If you can't find them, you can substitute 1½ cups chopped green onions and 2 tsp chopped garlic for 1 cup scapes.

Candied Onions and Fennel

MAKES ABOUT 2 CUPS

A delicious mixture to serve with lamb or anything else. It keeps for about two weeks in the refrigerator.

2 cups thinly sliced fennel	¼ cup balsamic vinegar
2 tbsp butter	¼ cup honey
4 cups thinly sliced Spanish onions	2 tbsp Scotch whisky
Salt and freshly ground pepper	

BRING a large pot of water to a boil. Add fennel and return to a boil. Boil for 1 minute and drain well.

HEAT butter in a large skillet over medium heat. Add onions and fennel and season well with salt and pepper. Sauté for 5 minutes, or until onions are softened.

ADD vinegar, honey and Scotch and bring to a boil. Reduce heat and simmer until the onions and fennel become caramelized and sticky, about 40 minutes. Taste and adjust seasonings if necessary.

{ sautéing and stir-frying }

Sautéing is a basic cooking technique common to all the world's cuisines. The French word *sauté* means to jump. It describes the technique of quickly flipping and turning food in a skillet to soften but not brown. Food can be cooked right through with this technique, but sautéing can also be a preliminary step before finishing the cooking in a liquid.

The sautéing technique is an advantage to the person who wants to cook fresh food quickly. Toss some thinly sliced meat, poultry or fish into a skillet, add a few vegetables, season well, and you'll have a meal in minutes.

Sautéing in French cooking becomes stir-frying in Asian cooking, but the method is the same. Sautéing and stir-frying both involve constant stirring and tossing.

Usually fairly high heat is used when sautéing meats, because if the fat is not hot enough, the juices will not be sealed in and will run into the pan, creating steam. Don't crowd the pan, because this will lower the pan temperature and cause the juices to run out.

Ideally you should heat the pan first (the food is less likely to stick). Then add the oil and heat it. Add ingredients to the hot oil and toss quickly to cook through but not brown.

Sautéed Snow Peas and Pine Nuts with Black Sesame Seeds

SERVES 4

A simple but very attractive side dish. I like to string snow peas, though lots of people don't bother. Either way is fine.

2 tbsp butter	2 tbsp orange juice
10 oz (300 g) snow peas, strings removed	1 tbsp black sesame seeds
¼ cup pine nuts	½ tsp grated orange rind
2 tbsp chicken stock or water	Salt and freshly ground pepper

HEAT butter in a large skillet over medium-high heat. Add snow peas and pine nuts and sauté for 1 to 2 minutes, or until snow peas are slightly softened.

STIR in stock and orange juice and bring to a boil. Boil for 2 minutes, or until sauce coats snow peas. Stir in sesame seeds and orange rind. Season with salt and pepper.

{ edible-podded peas }

Snow peas are available year round, but they have more flavour in the spring and summer. Choose firm, smooth, bright-green pods that do not have discernible peas inside. Before cooking, remove the string along the length of the pod by pinching it at the stem end and pulling it towards the tip. Steam or sauté snow peas, or boil in lots of water until tender-crisp.

Sugar snaps have fatter pods than snow peas and are also eaten whole, but the strings must be removed before cooking. They have a crisp, juicy texture and usually need a slightly longer cooking time than snow peas.

Spinach Gratin

SERVES 4

The perfect spinach dish—quite rich and great with chicken and beef roasts or grills.

2 large bunches spinach, trimmed	**Topping**
1 tbsp butter	1 tbsp butter, melted
½ cup whipping cream	½ cup fresh breadcrumbs
¼ tsp ground nutmeg	½ tsp finely chopped garlic
Salt and freshly ground pepper	Salt and freshly ground pepper

PREHEAT oven to 400 F.

WASH spinach and place in a pot or skillet over medium heat. Cover and steam until spinach wilts, about 5 minutes. Drain well, cool slightly and squeeze out as much water as possible. Chop spinach.

HEAT butter in a large skillet over medium heat. Add spinach and toss in butter to coat.

ADD cream and increase heat to medium-high. Boil for 5 minutes, or until cream reduces to about ⅓ cup (just enough to make a sauce for the spinach). Add nutmeg and season with salt and pepper. Spoon spinach mixture into a buttered gratin dish.

COMBINE melted butter, breadcrumbs and garlic in a small bowl. Season with salt and pepper. Sprinkle crumb mixture evenly over spinach.

BAKE for 20 minutes, or until juices are bubbling and top is lightly golden.

{ spinach }

Spinach needs to be rinsed even if it is prewashed when you buy it. Rinse it in warm water (better to dislodge the dirt), trim the stalks and place the spinach in a pot just with the water that clings to the leaves. Always squeeze the water out of spinach after it is cooked, or it will taste watery.

Baby spinach is easier to cook and doesn't need to be rinsed, but it has less flavour. I use it when I am in a hurry, or in stir-fries or sautéed dishes.

Braised Winter Greens

SERVES 4

Leafy greens have much to recommend them. They are packed with nutrients, full of iron and versatile—they can be prepared many ways and absorb seasonings beautifully.

Use escarole, frisee, endive, Swiss chard, beet tops, collard greens or a mixture, removing the tough stem ends if necessary. These greens are slightly bitter but mellow out when cooked.

1 lb (500 g) winter greens
3 tbsp olive oil
1 cup sliced shallots

½ cup vegetable or chicken stock
Salt and freshly ground pepper

BRING a pot of salted water to a boil. Add greens and boil for 2 minutes, or until greens are just tender. Drain well. Chop coarsely.

HEAT oil in a large skillet over medium-high heat. Add shallots and sauté for 1 minute.

ADD greens and stock and season with salt and pepper. Cover skillet and reduce heat to low. Cook for 5 minutes, or until greens are tender.

{ boiling vegetables }

A rule of thumb I learned at the esteemed Cordon Bleu cookery school is that vegetables that grow above the ground go into lots of boiling salted water and are boiled vigorously for a short time. Vegetables that grow beneath the ground go into cold salted water before being brought to a boil and are cooked covered, much like the dark place they grow. It's a good guide if you're ever in doubt.

Sautéed Fiddleheads Italian Style

SERVES 4

This recipe is the result of a discussion I had with Tony di Marco, owner of Harvest Wagon in Toronto. He persuaded me that fiddleheads could absorb these very Italian flavours. Serve this as a side dish or toss with short pasta.

8 oz (250 g) fiddleheads, washed	2 tbsp chopped anchovy fillets
2 tbsp olive oil	Pinch chili flakes
1 tbsp butter	1 tbsp balsamic vinegar
1 tsp chopped garlic	Salt and freshly ground pepper
¼ cup chopped sun-dried tomatoes	

BRING a pot of salted water to a boil. Add fiddleheads and boil for 4 to 5 minutes, or until tender-crisp. Refresh under cold water until cool and drain well.

HEAT oil and butter in a large skillet over medium heat. Add garlic, tomatoes and anchovies. Sauté for about 1 minute, or until garlic is softened.

STIR in fiddleheads and chili flakes and cook until fiddleheads have absorbed flavours, about 2 minutes. Sprinkle with balsamic vinegar. Season with salt and pepper only if needed.

{ fiddleheads }

Fiddleheads are the tightly rolled heads of the ostrich fern. They are available fresh in the spring. Because the heads are tightly rolled, they need to be cleaned very well. First shake them in a paper bag to remove the papery skin. Then wash them in several changes of water, swishing them around with your hands to release any soil in the fronds. Before using, cut off the tough brown part at the base of the fern.

Sichuan Eggplant

SERVES 4

This dark, sensuous dish makes a sensational accompaniment for simply prepared fish or chicken. Sichuan peppercorns are a fragrant, flowery-tasting Asian spice available at Asian markets, but if you don't have them, just omit.

½ cup soy sauce	1 tsp Sichuan peppercorns, optional
½ cup hoisin sauce	3 Japanese eggplants
1 tbsp hot Asian chili sauce	¼ cup vegetable oil
¼ cup seasoned rice vinegar	1 red pepper, thinly sliced
¼ cup sake	1 small onion, thinly sliced
2 tbsp chopped garlic	2 tbsp chopped garlic chives

COMBINE soy sauce, hoisin, chili sauce, vinegar, sake, garlic and peppercorns in a bowl.

CUT each eggplant in half lengthwise, then cut each half into 4 pieces.

HEAT a wok or large skillet over high heat. Add oil and heat. Add eggplants, red pepper and onion and stir-fry for 5 minutes.

COVER wok, reduce heat to medium-low and cook for 5 minutes, or until eggplant is soft.

ADD soy sauce mixture, increase heat to medium and simmer, uncovered, for 6 minutes, or until sauce is syrupy, stirring occasionally. Garnish with chives.

{ eggplant }

I prefer to use the long Japanese eggplants in many dishes. They do not need to be salted beforehand, and they cook quickly.

Another excellent eggplant is the football-shaped Sicilian eggplant, with its creamy interior and custard-like texture. Small Italian eggplants are also great for stuffing and baking. The small eggplants do not need to be salted.

Regular large eggplants should be salted before cooking to eliminate the bitter juices. Sprinkle the sliced or cubed eggplant with salt and let sit for an hour before cooking.

Sautéed Rapini

SERVES 4

Rapini has a peppery taste that is addictive. Serve it with chicken, lamb or salmon for a real flavour hit. It is also excellent tossed with pasta, especially orecchiette.

1 bunch rapini, trimmed	½ tsp chili flakes
2 tbsp olive oil	Salt and freshly ground pepper to taste
1 tsp chopped garlic	

BRING a large pot of salted water to a boil. Add rapini and boil for 4 minutes, or until tender-crisp. Refresh with cold water and drain well.

HEAT oil in a large skillet over medium heat. Add garlic, chili flakes and rapini and sauté until hot, about 2 minutes. Season with salt and pepper.

{ rapini }

Rapini is a leafy green vegetable with small broccoli-like florets. It is used in Italian cooking and a version of it, sometimes called Chinese flowering cabbage or Chinese broccoli, is used in Chinese cooking, too. It should be blanched before using, or it can be a bit bitter and tough.

{ blanching }

Blanching means immersing food in boiling water for a minute or two to partially cook it. To blanch a vegetable, bring a large pot of water to a boil. Add the vegetable and return to a boil. Boil for 1 minute, then drain and refresh in plenty of cold water until the vegetable is cold to stop the cooking and help retain the bright colour.

Grilled Portobello Mushrooms

SERVES 4

These are always good with chicken and steaks. Serve them warm or cold.

4 large portobello mushrooms, trimmed
¼ cup olive oil
Salt and freshly ground pepper

Garlic and Shallot Dressing
2 tbsp balsamic vinegar
2 tbsp finely chopped shallots
2 tsp minced garlic
¼ cup olive oil
Salt and freshly ground pepper

PREHEAT grill on high.

CUT mushrooms into slices ½ inch thick. Brush with oil and season with salt and pepper. Grill until tender, about 2 to 3 minutes per side.

WHISK vinegar, shallots and garlic in a small bowl. Whisk in olive oil. Season with salt and pepper. Toss mushrooms with dressing.

Grilled Green Onions

SERVES 4

I made this simple recipe at the cottage and was surprised by how much everyone liked it.

2 bunches green onions
1 tbsp olive oil

1 tbsp butter
Salt and freshly ground pepper

PREHEAT grill on high.

CLEAN onions, leaving roots intact. Place onions on a sheet of foil. Dot with oil, butter, salt and pepper. Wrap foil loosely to completely enclose onions.

GRILL onions for 6 minutes, turning once.

I often use a mix of fresh mushrooms to give greater depth to dishes.

CHANTERELLES • These funnel- or trumpet-shaped mushrooms only grow in the wild under hardwood trees. They have a peppery flavour with a slight hint of apricots, and they stand up well to being used with other ingredients. If they are dirty, brush them with a mushroom brush or soak them briefly in water and pat dry.

ENOKI • Enoki mushrooms look like waving seaweed and don't have much taste, but they make a beautiful garnish.

KING • Actually an oyster mushroom, king mushrooms have a meaty texture and are drier than other mushrooms. They are great in sautés and stir-fries. I usually use them on their own because they can overpower the taste and texture of other varieties.

MORELS • Morels are wild mushrooms with honeycomb caps that can retain a fair bit of soil. Although mushrooms normally should never be washed (brush or wipe them clean), morels need a good rinse before cooking. Dry them off immediately. They have a nutty, woodsy flavour that goes perfectly with chicken and beef.

OYSTER • These attractive mushrooms are good grilled and as part of a mixed mushroom dish, although they don't have much flavour. Instead of slicing them with a knife, try tearing them into strips.

PORTOBELLO AND CREMINI • Portobellos are large mushrooms with lots of flavour and a meaty texture. They are good grilled and make an interesting soup. Cut off the stems and remove the gills if the mushrooms are to be incorporated with other ingredients, as the gills leak a black juice that can spoil the look of a dish.

Cremini or brown mushrooms are small portobellos. They have a slightly deeper flavour than white mushrooms.

SHIITAKE • Originally from Japan, shiitakes are now grown here. They have a woodsy flavour and star in Asian dishes. Their fragrance perfumes rice, noodles and broths. Always remove the stems before cooking.

Glazed Carrots and Parsnips with Chives

SERVES 4 TO 6

A classic vegetable dish for holiday entertaining. You can also use all carrots or add turnips to the mix.

1 lb (500 g) carrots	2 tbsp lemon juice
1 lb (500 g) parsnips	½ cup chicken stock
3 tbsp butter	Salt and freshly ground pepper
½ cup orange juice	2 tbsp chopped chives

PEEL carrots and parsnips and cut into sticks about 3 inches long and ½ inch thick.

HEAT butter in a large skillet over medium heat. Add carrots and parsnips and sauté for 5 minutes, or until tinged with brown.

ADD orange juice, lemon juice and stock. Bring to a boil, reduce heat, cover and simmer for 8 to 10 minutes, or until vegetables are cooked. Uncover, increase heat and cook for 2 to 3 minutes, or until liquid is syrupy. Season with salt and pepper and sprinkle with chives.

Zucchini and Red Pepper Compote

SERVES 4

For a vibrant fall colour combination, use both yellow and green zucchini.

2 zucchini	2 tomatoes, seeded and diced
2 tbsp olive oil	2 tbsp shredded fresh basil
1 red pepper, seeded and diced	Salt and freshly ground pepper
½ tsp finely chopped garlic	

CUT zucchini in half lengthwise and slice.

HEAT oil in a large skillet over medium-high heat. Add zucchini and red pepper and sauté until vegetables are browned and slightly softened, about 5 to 6 minutes.

STIR in garlic, tomatoes and basil and bring to a boil. Season with salt and pepper.

Celery Root Latkes

As a change from potato latkes, try these flavourful and interesting pancakes. They are wonderful with lamb chops. You could also use half celery root and half potatoes.

4 cups grated celery root

½ cup grated onions, squeezed dry

1 egg, beaten

1 tsp ground cumin

¼ cup all-purpose flour

Salt and freshly ground pepper

¼ cup vegetable oil

COMBINE celery root, onions, egg and cumin in a bowl. Stir in flour and season well with salt and pepper.

HEAT a large non-stick skillet over medium heat. Add enough oil to cover base of skillet and heat.

DROP 2 tbsp batter into skillet for each pancake. Flatten with back of a spoon until about 3 inches in diameter. Fry for 2 to 3 minutes on each side, or until brown and crisp.

STIR batter before next batch, adding more oil to skillet as needed.

{ celery root }

Celery root (celeriac) is a gnarly bulbous vegetable with a taste similar to celery but with a much more usable texture for cooking. Peel and slice it for salads—it is the main ingredient in the famous French salad, celery root remoulade. It can be roasted, sautéed or grated into pancakes. For an interesting mash, combine it with other root vegetables such as Jerusalem artichokes or parsnips.

Baked Celery Root, Jerusalem Artichokes and Fingerling Potatoes

SERVES 8

A traditional rustic Italian way to cook vegetables. This looks best if all the vegetables are approximately the same size. If you can't find fingerlings, cut Yukon Golds into thick batons.

1 small celery root, peeled	Salt and freshly ground pepper
1 lb (500 g) Jerusalem artichokes, peeled	2 tsp chopped fresh thyme, or 1 tsp dried
1 lb (500 g) fingerling potatoes, scrubbed	2 tbsp butter
16 garlic cloves, peeled	2 tbsp olive oil

PREHEAT oven to 400 F.

CUT celery root into 2-inch pieces. Place in a bowl along with Jerusalem artichokes, potatoes and garlic cloves. Season well with salt, pepper and thyme.

HEAT butter and oil in a large skillet over medium heat. Add vegetables in batches and sauté until lightly coloured, about 4 to 5 minutes. Transfer vegetables to a large baking dish.

COVER dish with foil and bake for 30 minutes, shaking dish occasionally. Remove foil and cook for 10 minutes longer, or until vegetables are tender and golden.

{ jerusalem artichokes }

Jerusalem artichokes are not artichokes at all. They are a knobby root vegetable that looks a little like ginger but with an artichoke-like taste. Peel them with a potato peeler. They are excellent fried, thinly sliced and served raw or roasted. You can also mash them with potatoes.

Squash and Roasted Garlic Gratin

SERVES 6

This is one of my family's favourites. If you can buy roasted garlic puree, substitute ⅓ cup.

1 butternut squash, halved and seeded	¼ cup chopped parsley
1 tbsp olive oil	Salt and freshly ground pepper
2 garlic heads	½ cup fresh breadcrumbs
¼ cup butter	

PREHEAT oven to 400 F.

RUB cut side of squash with oil and place flesh side down on a parchment-lined baking sheet.

TRIM top third from heads of garlic. Brush cut sides with oil and wrap in foil. Bake squash and garlic for 45 minutes, or until tender.

SCRAPE squash flesh into a bowl. Squeeze garlic out of cloves and add to squash. Add 3 tbsp butter and parsley and beat until incorporated. Season well with salt and pepper.

SPOON squash into a buttered gratin dish, sprinkle with breadcrumbs, dot with remaining 1 tbsp butter and bake for 20 minutes.

{ making breadcrumbs }

To make breadcrumbs, use two-day-old bread with crusts, cut into even-sized pieces. For fresh breadcrumbs, place the bread in a food processor and process until crumbly. If fine crumbs are needed, spread fresh breadcrumbs on a baking sheet and bake at 200 F until dried, about 20 minutes. Reprocess until fine.

Store fresh breadcrumbs in plastic bags in the freezer. (They do not need to be defrosted before being used.)

Sweet Potato and Ginger Hash

SERVES 6

A tasty side dish that can be made ahead and reheated in the oven before serving.

3 sweet potatoes, peeled and cut in
   ½-inch cubes
2 tbsp vegetable oil
1 cup coarsely chopped onions

1 tbsp chopped gingerroot
1 tsp ground ginger
Salt and freshly ground pepper
2 tbsp chopped fresh mint

PLACE sweet potatoes in a pot and cover with cold salted water. Bring to a boil and boil until potatoes are partially cooked, about 2 minutes. Drain well.

HEAT oil in a large skillet over medium heat. Add onions and gingerroot and sauté until onions are just tinged with gold, about 3 minutes. Add ground ginger and stir to combine.

ADD sweet potatoes and continue to cook for about 3 minutes, or until golden brown. Season with salt and pepper and sprinkle with mint.

{ sweet potatoes, yams and boniato }

Is it a sweet potato or a yam? Actually, it is a sweet potato. Several decades ago, when orange-fleshed sweet potatoes were introduced in the southern United States, producers wanted to distinguish them from the more traditional, less-sweet white-fleshed potatoes. So they called them yams, an adaptation of the African word *nyami* (even though they have nothing to do with Africa). Sweet potatoes can be pale skinned with a lighter flesh or orange fleshed with a darker skin. They are low in calories and full of vitamins. Keep them in a cool place, but not refrigerated—their flavour will go off.

True yams are South American and have a brown or black skin. The flesh is usually off-white, but it can be purple or red as well (purple potatoes are, in fact, yams). They have a fluffier texture and less-sweet taste than sweet potatoes. The South American name is boniato, and they can be found in Caribbean and South American grocery stores.

Stir-fried Bok Choy with Shiitake Mushrooms

SERVES 6

A great-tasting side that reheats well in the microwave.

2 tbsp vegetable oil

2 tsp chopped garlic

1 tbsp chopped gingerroot

6 cups baby bok choy, trimmed

6 oz (175 g) shiitake mushrooms, stemmed and
thickly sliced

$\frac{1}{3}$ cup chicken stock or water

2 tbsp soy sauce

1 tsp granulated sugar

Salt and freshly ground pepper

HEAT a wok or large skillet over high heat. Add oil and heat. Add garlic and ginger and stir-fry for 30 seconds.

ADD bok choy and mushrooms and stir-fry for 3 to 4 minutes, or until mushrooms are tender.

ADD stock, soy sauce and sugar. Bring to a boil and cook for about 2 minutes, or until liquid glazes vegetables. Season with salt and pepper.

Braised Red Cabbage

SERVES 8

A winner with roasted pork or poultry. This dish reheats and freezes well, making it perfect for large-scale entertaining (it actually tastes better the day after you make it).

1 medium red cabbage, shredded	Salt and freshly ground pepper
1 tsp salt	1 bay leaf
2 tbsp butter	3 whole cloves
1 tbsp vegetable oil	1 cup red wine
1 large red onion, chopped	2 tbsp red wine vinegar
2 apples, peeled and chopped	2 tbsp brown sugar
1 tsp chopped garlic	

SPRINKLE cabbage with salt and let sit for 30 minutes. Drain well.

HEAT butter and oil in a large skillet or pot over medium-high heat. Add onions and apples and sauté until softened, about 2 to 3 minutes.

ADD cabbage and garlic and sauté for about 4 minutes, or until coated with oil. Season with salt, pepper, bay leaf and cloves.

ADD wine, vinegar and sugar. Bring to a boil, stirring occasionally. Reduce heat to low, cover and cook for 45 to 60 minutes, or until cabbage is tender. Taste and adjust seasonings if necessary. Remove bay leaf before serving.

Shredded Brussels Sprouts with Pine Nuts and Prosciutto

SERVES 4

Because the shredded sprouts don't look like Brussels sprouts, this is a good dish for people who are reluctant to try them.

Occasionally I stir in some grated Fontina or provolone cheese just before serving.

1 lb (500 g) Brussels sprouts
¼ cup olive oil
4 slices prosciutto, chopped

½ cup toasted pine nuts
Salt and freshly ground pepper

TRIM root ends and cores from Brussels sprouts. Cut sprouts in half and slice thinly.

HEAT oil in a large skillet over medium-high heat. Add prosciutto and sauté for 2 to 3 minutes, or until beginning to crisp. Add sprouts and sauté for 3 minutes.

COVER skillet, reduce heat to low and cook for 2 minutes longer, or until sprouts are tender-crisp.

ADD pine nuts and cook for 1 minute. Season with salt and pepper.

Roasted Cauliflower with Mustard Seeds

SERVES 6

Indian flavourings add a dynamic taste to cauliflower. Serve this with plain roast chicken or pork or other Indian dishes. You can also make it ahead and reheat in a 350 F oven for about 10 minutes before serving.

1 cauliflower, cut in small florets (about 10 cups)	1 tbsp lemon juice
3 tbsp vegetable oil	1/4 cup plain yogurt
1 tbsp mustard seeds	Salt and freshly ground pepper
2 tsp cumin seeds	

PREHEAT oven to 450 F.

TOSS cauliflower with 2 tbsp oil. Spread on a baking sheet and roast for 8 minutes. Turn and cook for 7 to 10 minutes longer, or until tender-crisp.

HEAT remaining 1 tbsp oil in a large skillet over high heat. Add mustard and cumin seeds and stir-fry for 1 minute, or until seeds begin to pop. Add cauliflower, reduce heat to medium-low and toss together for 1 minute, or until cauliflower is coated with seeds.

STIR in lemon juice and yogurt. Season with salt and pepper.

{ mustard seeds }

Mustard seeds come in three colours. Black, the most flavourful, are used in Indian cooking, usually in vegetable dishes. Brown, which are piquant and sharp tasting, are used to make Dijon mustard and are grown in Canada. Yellow, the mildest seeds, are used in pickling and to make American mustard.

{ quickbreads, cookies and bars }

Magic Morning Muffins

MAKES 24 MUFFINS

We call these magic because they are moist and flavourful as well as being good for you. They stay fresh for about three days. This recipe makes two dozen muffins, but they are not large, and they freeze well.

This recipe calls for natural bran instead of processed bran cereal. The flavour will be much better if the bran is toasted.

3 cups natural bran	2 tsp grated lemon rind
1 cup pitted prunes	1/2 cup all-purpose flour
1/2 cup water	1/2 cup whole wheat flour
1 1/2 cups buttermilk	1 1/2 tsp baking soda
2 eggs	1/2 tsp baking powder
3/4 cup vegetable oil	1/2 tsp salt
3/4 cup brown sugar	1/2 cup raisins or dried cranberries

PREHEAT oven to 350 F.

SPREAD bran on a baking sheet and bake for 6 minutes, or until fragrant.

PREPARE prunes while bran is toasting. Combine prunes and water in a small pot over medium heat. Bring to a boil and simmer for 7 minutes, or until prunes are very soft and most of the liquid has been absorbed. Transfer prunes and any remaining water to a food processor and puree.

COMBINE prune puree, buttermilk, eggs, oil, sugar and lemon rind in a bowl.

COMBINE bran, both flours, baking soda, baking powder and salt in a separate large bowl. Add wet ingredients and stir until just combined. Stir in raisins.

SPOON batter into oiled or paper-lined medium muffin cups. Bake for 20 minutes, or until a toothpick inserted into muffin comes out clean.

Muffins have somehow acquired a healthy, low-calorie label, but beware—they are not necessarily low calorie, nor are they necessarily healthy. They are, however, very easy to make.

A good muffin has a dense but moist interior and is quite crumbly. Make sure the dry ingredients are well mixed. My colleague and recipe tester Eshun Mott says it's best to sift all the ingredients into the bowl, but, being lazy, I usually just stir everything together.

When you combine the wet and dry ingredients, the secret is not to overmix. Batter that is overmixed produces muffins with a dense, dry texture. Combine just until the dry ingredients are moistened. Don't worry about any lumps; they'll disappear in the baking.

The size of muffin cups varies. Whether you use large or small ones, all that changes is the baking time. Grease them well with butter or oil, or use paper baking cups. Fill the cups no more than three-quarters full to leave room for rising. If you have empty muffin cups left in the pan, fill them halfway with water to protect the pan from burning and help the muffins bake more evenly.

Bake muffins in the centre of the oven for even baking. After baking, remove them from the muffin cups immediately and cool on a wire rack or serve warm. Store them in plastic bags to help maintain moisture, or freeze them.

Dried Cherry Muffins

MAKES 12 MUFFINS

This is an outstanding and unusual muffin. The beer gives it a moist and cakey texture but does not affect the taste.

$3/4$ cup dried cherries	$1/2$ tsp baking soda
1 cup flat beer	$1/2$ tsp salt
2 cups all-purpose flour	$1/2$ cup butter, melted
1 cup granulated sugar	1 egg, beaten
1 tsp baking powder	$1/2$ cup chopped almonds

COMBINE cherries and beer in a small pot. Bring to a boil. Remove from heat and let sit for 30 minutes. Drain, reserving cherries and beer separately.

PREHEAT oven to 400 F.

COMBINE flour, sugar, baking powder, baking soda and salt in a large bowl.

COMBINE melted butter, egg and $1/2$ cup reserved beer in a separate bowl. Add wet ingredients to dry, gently stirring together (batter will be quite thick and may be a bit lumpy). Stir in reserved cherries and almonds.

FILL oiled or paper-lined muffin cups and bake for 16 to 18 minutes, or until a toothpick inserted in centre comes out clean.

Dill and Fennel Scones

MAKES 12 SCONES

These savoury scones can be made by hand or in a food processor. If you are using a food processor, stir in the milk by hand.

Serve these as a bread with dinner or as a base for smoked salmon, cheese or pâté. Make mini scones as an hors d'oeuvre (bake for 8 to 10 minutes) and top with fig chutney and Brie or other cheese.

2 ¼ cups all-purpose flour	½ cup chopped fresh dill
1 tbsp baking powder	1 tsp cracked fennel seeds
1 tsp salt	6 tbsp milk
¾ cup butter, cubed	

PREHEAT oven to 425 F.

SIFT flour, baking powder and salt into a large bowl. Cut in butter and sprinkle with dill and fennel. Work dough with your fingers until mixture resembles breadcrumbs.

ADD milk and mix with a fork or your fingers until dough just forms a ball. Do not overmix, or biscuits will be tough.

PLACE dough on a floured board and knead for 1 minute. Roll or pat out until ¾ inch thick.

CUT into 3-inch rounds and arrange on an ungreased baking sheet. Bake for 10 to 12 minutes, or until golden.

{ fresh scones }

If you use a food processor to make scones and biscuits, make sure you don't over-process the flour and butter mixture, or your scones will be dry and tough. For the freshest scones, measure the ingredients ahead of time but don't mix them together until just before baking. Or make the scones ahead and reheat in a 350 F oven for 5 minutes before serving.

Scottish Oatmeal Biscuits

MAKES ABOUT 20 BISCUITS

These biscuits, a particular favourite of mine, go superbly with smoked salmon, cheese or butter and marmalade. If you omit the baking powder, the texture will be crisper. You can also make them thinner than specified in the recipe; just reduce the baking time.

3 cups quick-cooking rolled oats
1 ½ cups all-purpose flour
2 tbsp granulated sugar
2 tsp baking powder

1 ½ tsp baking soda
1 ½ tsp salt
1 cup butter, cubed
¼ cup water

PREHEAT oven to 325 F.

COMBINE rolled oats, flour, sugar, baking powder, baking soda and salt in a large bowl. Cut in butter until mixture resembles small peas.

STIR in enough water to bring dough together and knead gently. Roll or pat out dough on a lightly floured surface until about ½ inch thick.

CUT out biscuits using a 3-inch cookie cutter. Place on an ungreased baking sheet.

BAKE for 25 minutes, or until bottoms are lightly browned. Biscuits will crisp as they cool. Remove from baking sheets and cool on rack.

Walnut Cracker Bread

SERVES 10

This crunchy, easy-to-make cracker bread keeps very well in an airtight tin, but I like to reheat it for 5 minutes in a 350 F oven to make sure it is nice and crisp before serving. It makes a great afternoon snack or little nibble with drinks and is superb with cheese. The seeds and nuts can be altered to your taste.

3 cups all-purpose flour
2 tbsp granulated sugar
1 tsp kosher salt
1 cup butter, cubed
1 tsp fennel seeds
1 cup chopped walnuts
¾ cup water

Topping
1 egg, beaten
1 tsp kosher or Maldon salt

COMBINE flour, sugar, salt, butter, fennel and walnuts in a food processor. Process until butter is size of peas.

BLEND in enough water to bring dough together (you may need slightly more or less than ¾ cup).

TRANSFER dough to a bowl and knead lightly until it forms a ball. Flatten dough into a disc and wrap in plastic wrap. Chill for 30 minutes.

PREHEAT oven to 350 F.

DIVIDE dough into four pieces. Roll out each piece as thinly as possible on a floured surface (shape can be irregular). Transfer to ungreased baking sheets and prick with a fork. Brush with beaten egg and sprinkle with salt.

BAKE in centre of oven (you may have to bake these one at a time) for 18 minutes, or until golden and crisp. Cool on a rack. Break up crackers into smaller pieces.

My Favourite Shortbread

MAKES ABOUT 36 COOKIES

Although I keep searching for the ultimate shortbread recipe, I always come back to this one that I have been making for years. It is a true Scottish shortbread made with rice flour, which provides the fine, crumbly texture associated with good shortbread. Store the cookies in an airtight container for up to two weeks.

³/₄ cup granulated sugar	1 tsp salt
3 cups all-purpose flour	2 cups butter, cubed
³/₄ cup rice flour	

PREHEAT oven to 325 F.

PROCESS sugar in a food processor for 30 seconds. Add flours and salt and process until combined.

ADD butter and pulse for about 30 seconds, or until mixture resembles fresh breadcrumbs.

TRANSFER dough to a lightly floured surface and knead for about 2 minutes, or until a ball is formed.

ROLL out dough until ½ inch thick. Cut out cookies using a 2-inch cookie cutter dipped in flour. Arrange cookies on ungreased baking sheets and prick with a fork.

BAKE cookies for 13 to 15 minutes, or until a creamy colour. If cookies are browning too quickly, reduce heat to 300 F.

Ginger Pecan Thins

MAKES ABOUT 50 COOKIES

The dough for these cookies can be made ahead and frozen. Defrost the logs in the refrigerator, then slice and bake whenever you want a batch of freshly baked cookies.

$1/2$ cup crystallized ginger
2 $1/4$ cups all-purpose flour
1 cup butter, at room temperature
1 cup icing sugar

1 egg
Pinch salt
1 cup coarsely chopped pecans

COMBINE ginger and $1/4$ cup flour in a food processor and pulse until ginger is finely chopped. (Do not overprocess, or mixture will become pasty.)

CREAM butter and sugar in a bowl, by hand or with an electric mixer until light and fluffy. Beat in egg until well incorporated.

COMBINE remaining 2 cups flour, salt and pecans in a separate bowl. Stir into creamed mixture along with chopped ginger.

DIVIDE dough into thirds and form into logs about 2 inches in diameter. Wrap logs in wax paper and chill for 4 hours, or until firm.

PREHEAT oven to 375 F.

SLICE chilled dough as thinly as possible (between $1/8$ inch and $1/4$ inch thick) and place on buttered baking sheets.

BAKE for 8 to 10 minutes, or until edges are golden. Cool on racks. Store in airtight cookie tins.

{ crystallized ginger }

Crystallized ginger is gingerroot that has been cooked in a sugar syrup, air-dried and rolled in sugar. It is also called candied ginger. Look for it in health food stores and supermarkets (buy the superior Australian product if you can find it). Preserved ginger is more difficult to find. The ginger is cooked and preserved in a heavy sugar syrup. It is sold in jars.

{ baking cookies }

Drop cookies (such as chocolate chip) are the easiest cookies to make; just drop the soft dough onto baking sheets by the spoonful. They spread as they bake, so be sure to leave about 2 inches between them. The baked cookies will be crisper if they are removed from the baking sheet after a couple of minutes and dried on racks. If they cool directly on the sheets, they will be chewier. Shortbread and delicate cookies must be left on the baking sheets until cool—otherwise they will break.

For rolled cookies, such as shortbread, the dough is rolled out on a floured, smooth surface and cut into shapes with a cookie cutter or knife, then baked. The cookies do not spread when cooking, so you can place them close together.

Ice box, or refrigerator, cookies are made from dough that has been formed into logs, chilled and then cut into thick or thin slices. They are generally crisper than other cookies, and you can prepare the dough ahead of time. Roll the dough into logs, wrap well and chill for up to a week before baking, or freeze. They do not spread when baked.

Place the baking sheet on the middle rack of the oven for even baking. If you are using more than one rack, switch the position of the baking sheets after they have baked for half the baking time. If you do not have heavy or insulated baking sheets, stack two sheets together to protect the bottoms of delicate cookies from burning.

Grease baking sheets lightly with oil or unsalted butter, spray with non-stick coating or line them with parchment paper for easy cleanup. (Shortbread cookies and other cookies containing lots of butter are usually baked on ungreased baking sheets.) Don't bother regreasing baking sheets between batches; just wipe off any crumbs with a paper towel.

French Macaroons

MAKES ABOUT 60 MACAROONS OR 30 SANDWICH COOKIES

Macaroons are the classic meringue cookies that have lately taken Paris by storm. They can be made large or small (I like them small) and filled with every conceivable flavouring, from green tea and fruit to herb pastes.

I like to fill macaroons with white and dark chocolate ganache, a rich chocolate filling used in cakes, pastries and truffles. (Roll any leftover ganache into balls for homemade truffles.)

For chocolate macaroons, fold ½ cup cocoa into the meringue mixture (I often divide the meringue mixture and make half chocolate and half white macaroons).

4 egg whites	1 cup ground almonds
1 cup granulated sugar	1 cup white chocolate ganache
2 tsp white vinegar	1 cup dark chocolate ganache

PREHEAT oven to 300 F.

BEAT egg whites in a large bowl with an electric mixer until foamy. Gradually beat in ½ cup sugar. Continue to beat on high speed for about 4 minutes, or until very thick and glossy and mixture holds stiff peaks. Add vinegar and beat for 1 minute.

COMBINE remaining sugar and ground almonds in a small bowl. Gently fold into egg whites until just combined.

USE a piping bag with a plain tip to pipe macaroons onto parchment-lined baking sheets. Ideally macaroons are about the diameter of a toonie, nicely mounded without peaks or points (this takes some practice). Push any peaks down with a wet knife. You can also dollop them onto baking sheet with a tablespoon—not as pretty, but they will taste the same.

BAKE macaroons for 20 minutes. Turn off oven and leave them for 30 minutes longer. They should be pale gold. Remove macaroons from oven and transfer to a rack to cool.

PLACE a spoonful of ganache on flat side of one meringue and sandwich together with a second meringue. Repeat until all ingredients are used.

DARK CHOCOLATE GANACHE • Bring ¾ cup whipping cream to a boil in a small pot. Remove from heat. Add 4 oz (125 g) coarsely chopped bittersweet chocolate and stir until melted. Stir in 2 tbsp butter. Allow to cool, stirring occasionally, until ganache is firm enough to spread.

Makes about 1 cup.

WHITE CHOCOLATE GANACHE • Bring ½ cup whipping cream to a boil in a small pot. Remove from heat. Add 6 oz (175 g) coarsely chopped white chocolate and stir until melted. Stir in 2 tbsp butter. Allow to cool, stirring occasionally, until ganache is firm enough to spread.

Makes about 1 cup.

{ working with egg whites }

SEPARATING EGG WHITES • Although there are special gadgets for separating eggs, the easiest method is to use your hands. Crack the shell and break the egg into your closed hand. Place your hand over a bowl and open your fingers slightly. The white will drip through. You can also crack the shell in half and then pass the yolk from one shell to the other, letting the white fall into a bowl. If some yolk drops into the bowl, the oil in the yolk will prevent the egg whites from whipping. Spoon out the yolk with the egg shell.

BEATING EGG WHITES • For meringues, egg whites should be beaten until they are thick and glossy and hold stiff peaks. They should be firm enough to support an egg in the shell (a more practical test than the popular but dangerous method of holding the bowl upside down to see whether the whites are firm enough not to fall out!).

If your beaten egg whites look dry and flaky, they have probably been overbeaten. They have lost their elasticity and won't hold as much air. The remedy is to add another white and continue beating until the mixture holds stiff peaks.

FOLDING EGG WHITES • Folding is the process of gently combining a lighter mixture with a heavier one (as in a cake batter) so as not to dislodge any air and deflate the mixture. Folding beaten egg whites must be done carefully and quickly to retain lightness and air.

First, stir one-quarter of the beaten egg whites into the heavier mixture to lighten it. Spoon the remaining egg whites on top of the heavier mixture. Using the largest spoon or spatula you have (professional chefs often use their hands), cut down through the centre of the heavy mixture to the bottom of the bowl. Turn the spoon parallel to the surface of the bowl and bring it up along the side, turning the bowl slightly as you work. Continue lifting a layer of heavy mixture over the lighter one, using as few strokes as possible, until almost evenly combined.

Giant Chocoholic Chunk Cookies

MAKES ABOUT 20 3-INCH COOKIES

This is the definitive chocolate chip cookie, with chocolate in the dough and chocolate chunks distributed throughout the cookie. It is always the first to go on a tray of mixed cookies.

½ cup butter

12 oz (375 g) bittersweet chocolate, cut in small chunks

1 ½ cups all-purpose flour

½ tsp baking powder

½ tsp salt

2 eggs

1 ½ cups granulated sugar

2 tsp vanilla

PREHEAT oven to 350 F.

MELT butter and 4 oz (125 g) chocolate chunks in a heavy pot over low heat, stirring until smooth. Remove from heat and cool slightly.

COMBINE flour, baking powder and salt in a bowl.

COMBINE eggs, sugar and vanilla in a large bowl. Blend in chocolate mixture.

ADD flour mixture to egg mixture and stir in. Stir in remaining 8 oz (250 g) chocolate chunks.

DROP dough onto parchment-lined baking sheets in mounds of about 2 tbsp, 2 inches apart.

BAKE for 12 to 15 minutes, or until cookies are glossy, cracked on surface and soft inside. Do not overbake. Remove cookies from baking sheet and let cool on a wire rack.

Macadamia Nut Turtles

MAKES ABOUT 24

I watched these disappear at a party long before the other desserts. The rich, fatty taste of the macadamia nuts goes perfectly with the chocolate and caramel. You can also use mini marshmallows instead of caramels.

1 lb (500 g) bittersweet or milk chocolate, chopped	1 cup macadamia nuts, halved
	1 cup coarsely chopped caramels

HEAT chocolate in a heavy pot over low heat and cook, stirring occasionally, until chocolate melts.

STIR in macadamia nuts and caramels. Remove from heat. Drop onto parchment-lined baking sheets in mounds of about 1 tbsp. Refrigerate until firm.

Broken Cookie Bars

MAKES ABOUT 32 BARS

This instant dessert was developed by my mother, who would buy bargain bags of broken cookies at the supermarket and then look for ways to use them up. Crush the cookies in a food processor for a finer crumb, or hand chop for a coarser texture. If you have a bunch of mixed cookies in the cupboard, use any flavour combination you like. I personally like orange cookies.

8 oz (250 g) bittersweet chocolate, chopped	2 cups broken cookies
1 cup butter, cubed	1 cup chopped nuts, optional

HEAT chocolate and butter in a heavy pot over low heat. Cook together until melted. Remove from heat and stir in cookies and nuts.

SPREAD mixture in a buttered 8-inch square pan. Refrigerate until firm. Cut into bars.

Muskoka Bars

MAKES ABOUT 32 BARS

These are so easy to make and taste superb. They are similar to thin Nanaimo bars but taste much better.

This recipe uses storebought shortbread for the base. If the butter seems to separate out of the base when baked, don't worry; it will be reabsorbed. I keep the bars in the freezer to defrost for unexpected guests, although my daughter Emma says they also taste wonderful frozen.

Base
1/2 cup butter
1/3 cup cocoa powder
1/4 cup granulated sugar
1 egg
2 cups shortbread or other cookie crumbs

Middle Layer
1/4 cup butter
8 oz (250 g) white chocolate, chopped
1/2 cup unsweetened desiccated coconut
2 tsp grated lemon rind

Top Layer
3 oz (90 g) bittersweet chocolate, melted

PREHEAT oven to 350 F.

COMBINE butter, cocoa and sugar in a heavy pot over low heat and cook for a few minutes until butter melts. Remove from heat and add egg, stirring until well blended.

COMBINE cocoa mixture and cookie crumbs in a bowl and mix together thoroughly.

PAT mixture into a parchment-lined 8-inch square cake pan and bake for 10 minutes, or until the mixture looks dry. Cool.

PREPARE middle layer by combining butter and white chocolate in a small pot over low heat. Stir for a few minutes until chocolate melts. Stir in coconut and lemon rind. Spread over base. Cool.

DRIZZLE melted bittersweet chocolate over white chocolate layer in an attractive pattern. Refrigerate until firm. Cut into bars.

Coconut, Lime and Passionfruit Squares

MAKES 16 SQUARES

This popular dessert from Australia combines exotic fruit with a traditional pastry base. Buy ripe passionfruit (they will have an intense passionfruit smell), but if fresh are unavailable, look for small cans of passionfruit puree in Asian grocery stores or gourmet shops. You can also use pureed mango, but the taste will not be as concentrated.

Base
1 cup all-purpose flour
1 tbsp granulated sugar
¼ tsp baking powder
¼ tsp salt
½ cup butter, cubed

Filling
4 eggs
1 cup granulated sugar
¼ cup all-purpose flour
½ cup coconut milk
½ cup whipping cream
½ cup passionfruit pulp (about 6 passionfruit)
⅓ cup unsweetened desiccated coconut
1 tbsp grated lime rind
1 tbsp lime juice
¼ cup icing sugar

PREHEAT oven to 350 F.

SIFT flour, sugar, baking powder and salt in a bowl. Cut in butter until mixture resembles fresh breadcrumbs. (Alternatively, place all ingredients in a food processor and process until mixture is crumbly.)

PAT mixture into a parchment- or foil-lined 8-inch square cake pan. Bake for 20 minutes.

PREPARE filling by beating eggs and sugar in a bowl with an electric beater until slightly thickened and creamy. Beat in flour.

BEAT in coconut milk, cream, passionfruit, coconut, lime rind and juice. Pour over pastry.

BAKE for 35 to 45 minutes, or until set. Cool. Sprinkle with sifted icing sugar and cut into squares.

{ pastries and cakes }

Shortcrust Pastry

MAKES ENOUGH PASTRY FOR A 9- OR 10-INCH TWO-CRUST PIE

Use all butter if trans fat–free shortening is not available. And I always use unsalted butter, as it contains less water than salted butter.

This pastry works well with any savoury or fruit pie.

3 cups all-purpose flour	¼ cup trans fat–free shortening, cubed
1 tsp salt	⅓ cup cold water
¾ cup butter, cubed	1 tbsp white vinegar or lemon juice

HAND METHOD

SIFT flour and salt into a large bowl. Cut in butter and shortening with a pastry cutter (or rub together with your fingertips) until mixture resembles coarse breadcrumbs.

COMBINE water and vinegar in a measuring cup. Stir enough liquid into flour to gather dough into a ball. Knead dough for 1 minute. Divide dough into two portions and flatten slightly. Wrap in plastic wrap and refrigerate until needed.

FOOD PROCESSOR METHOD

ADD flour, salt, butter and shortening to a food processor. Pulse together until coarse crumbs form.

ADD liquid and pulse briefly, but do not allow dough to form a ball in processor. Transfer to a bowl and knead together by hand. Divide dough into two portions and flatten slightly. Wrap in plastic wrap and refrigerate until needed.

{ fat for pastry }

Butter makes the best-tasting pastry, but it doesn't give you that flaky, melt-in-your-mouth texture. I no longer use regular shortening, because it contains trans fats. Instead I look for organic or trans fat–free shortening. It can be difficult to find (look for it in health food stores and organic supermarkets), but it makes an excellent flaky pastry. I like to use 75 percent butter and 25 percent organic shortening if I can; otherwise I use all butter.

Lard makes a tasty pastry with the best texture. It has fallen into disfavour because it is animal fat, but it is becoming popular again, particularly non-hydrogenated lard.

In general, the higher the proportion of fat, the crisper and tastier the pastry. However, pastries with a high proportion of fat are more difficult to roll out. I usually pat high-fat pastry into the pan instead of rolling it, or I roll it out between two sheets of plastic wrap.

Sweet Pastry

MAKES ENOUGH PASTRY FOR A 9- OR 10-INCH SINGLE-CRUST PIE

Use this pastry for open-face fruit tarts and custard-based tarts. It is similar to shortbread in taste and can be patted into the pan instead of being rolled out. Because it has a high sugar content, it is baked just until it turns pale gold; if it is baked too long, the sugar will caramelize and the pastry will taste burnt.

This pastry is best made by hand.

1 ½ cups all-purpose flour	1 cup butter, cubed
3 tbsp granulated sugar	1 egg yolk
½ tsp salt	2 tbsp lemon juice or water

SIFT flour, sugar and salt into a bowl. Add butter and rub flour and butter together with your fingertips or cut in with a pastry cutter until mixture resembles coarse breadcrumbs.

COMBINE egg yolk and lemon juice in a measuring cup. Sprinkle over flour mixture and blend in. Gather into a ball and chill until needed.

{ baking blind }

Baking blind means prebaking the bottom crust to prevent the filling from making the crust soggy. Baking blind also stops the pastry from shrinking down the sides of the pie plate. Except for fruit pies, I usually prebake all single-crust pie shells for 15 minutes to prevent soggy crusts and leaky fillings.

To bake blind, place a piece of parchment paper or foil over the pastry after it has been fitted into the pie plate. The paper should extend about 1 inch beyond the rim of the pan.

Fill the paper to the top with pie weights (stainless-steel weights the size of peas) or dried beans.

Bake the pastry at 425 F for 15 minutes. Lift out the paper and the beans. (Store the beans in a container to reuse. They keep for years.) The partially baked pie shell can now be used for quiches or custard fillings.

If a recipe calls for a fully baked pie shell, reduce the oven temperature to 350 F after the initial 15 minutes and continue to bake for 10 minutes, or until the bottom is crisp and pale gold.

The first rule in pastry-making is not to be nervous. The hands of nervous pastry makers are warm and sweaty, and heat is the bane of perfect dough. The second rule is to handle the dough lightly so as not to overwork the gluten, the protein in flour that gives structure to the dough. If the dough is overworked or if heat is introduced, the gluten expands too much and the dough becomes tough and elastic.

Make sure the liquid and fat are cold. Unless you are using a food processor, the fat should be cold but not too hard, otherwise it will not blend properly with the flour. Remove the fat from the refrigerator about an hour before using and cut it into ½-inch cubes. (If you are using a food processor, the fat should be very cold—straight out of the refrigerator.)

Cut the fat into the flour with a pastry cutter or your fingertips until the mixture resembles coarse breadcrumbs. Sprinkle the cold liquid over the fat/flour mixture, adding only enough to hold the dough together. Don't worry if you can still see tiny pieces of fat—the pastry will be even flakier.

Gather the dough into a ball with your fingers. It should hold together but not feel sticky. If your dough becomes too elastic and difficult to roll, cover it with plastic wrap and refrigerate it for 30 minutes to relax the gluten.

To roll out pastry, cut the dough into two pieces. Lightly flour a large area of the counter or pastry board and the top of the dough. Flatten the dough a little by pressing down with the rolling pin.

Always starting in the centre, roll gently to the edges of the pastry, using light but firm strokes. Occasionally turn the pastry to keep it from sticking to the counter.

Roll the pastry until it is about ⅛ inch thick and large enough to fit your pie plate. Allow at least a ½-inch overhang.

To transfer the pastry to the pan, dust the rolling pin lightly with flour, then roll the pastry gently around the rolling pin. Unroll it over the pie plate and press snugly into the pan. If the pastry tears or you have gaps, moisten the spot with a drop of water and patch with some extra pastry.

Cut away the excess pastry, leaving a ½-inch overhang if you are making a pie with a pastry top.

Unless you are baking blind (page 237), chill the bottom crust in the refrigerator until the filling and top crust are ready. Roll out the top crust. Spoon the filling into the chilled bottom crust.

Moisten the bottom crust around the rim. Transfer the top crust to the pie and then press the bottom and top crusts together. Trim the excess pastry before pinching or fluting the edges together. Make steam vents by cutting slits or a design into the top crust with a knife.

Always bake the pie in the lower third of the oven to make sure the bottom crust is properly cooked.

Apple Cranberry Maple Crumb Tart

SERVES 6

A pastry base and crumb topping give this tart much flavour and texture. For an apple crumble, just omit the base.

½ recipe shortcrust pastry (page 236)
2 lb (1 kg) Spy or other tart apples
1 cup dried cranberries
¼ cup maple syrup
¼ cup granulated sugar
1 tbsp all-purpose flour

Topping
1 cup rolled oats
½ cup all-purpose flour
½ cup brown sugar
⅓ cup butter, cubed

PREHEAT oven to 425 F.

ROLL out pastry to fit a 9-inch pie plate. Chill pastry while preparing filling.

PEEL and slice apples and combine with cranberries in a large bowl.

COMBINE maple syrup, granulated sugar and flour in a small bowl. Pour over apple mixture and toss to coat fruit. Spoon fruit into pastry shell.

COMBINE rolled oats, flour and brown sugar in a food processor or bowl. Cut in butter until mixture resembles coarse breadcrumbs. Sprinkle topping over fruit.

BAKE for 15 minutes. Reduce heat to 350 F and bake for 35 to 45 minutes longer, or until filling is bubbling and pastry is golden.

{ thickening pie fillings }

Quick-cooking tapioca, cornstarch and flour are all used to thicken pie

fillings. I think tapioca is the best thickener for pies because it keeps the filling clear and bright. It is also unaffected by acids (which can impede thickening). Cornstarch gives a glossy look but adds an unnatural jellylike texture to fillings. Flour works as well, but it can leave an uncooked-flour taste in the filling if it is not cooked long enough.

Pear Tarte Tatin

SERVES 6

Tarte tatin is an upside-down tart made with the pastry on top of the fruit instead of underneath. This recipe for individual tarts is very easy to make. Substitute apples for the pears if desired. Serve the tarts with vanilla ice cream.

½ recipe shortcrust pastry (page 236)
½ cup softened butter

¾ cup granulated sugar
6 ripe pears, peeled and cored

PREHEAT oven to 400 F.

ROLL out pastry and cut six rounds to fit top of six 1-cup ramekins. Refrigerate rounds until needed.

DIVIDE butter among ramekins. Top with sugar.

SLICE pears thinly and arrange over butter/sugar mixture, filling each ramekin.

PLACE ramekins on a baking sheet and bake until pears are soft and slightly golden, about 40 minutes. Reduce heat to 350 F.

PLACE a round of pastry on each ramekin. (If the pears are very juicy, pour off some of the liquid before adding the pastry.) Bake for 20 minutes longer, or until pastry is cooked through and pears are slightly caramelized. Cool for 5 minutes.

TURN out onto serving plates so pastry is on bottom.

Peach Pie

SERVES 6 TO 8

This classic double-crust fruit pie is one of my daughter-in-law Natalie's favourite desserts. Change the fruit to plums or apples and/or add 2 tbsp chopped crystallized ginger to the filling.

1 recipe shortcrust pastry (page 236)
1 cup granulated sugar
3 tbsp all-purpose flour

6 cups peeled and sliced peaches
2 tbsp lemon juice
2 tbsp butter, diced

PREHEAT oven to 425 F.

ROLL one portion of dough into a 10-inch circle on a lightly floured board. Drape over rolling pin and transfer to a 9-inch pie plate. Trim excess pastry, leaving a ½-inch overhang.

ROLL remaining dough into a 10-inch circle and refrigerate until needed.

COMBINE sugar, flour, peaches and lemon juice in a large bowl. Pile into bottom crust and dot with butter.

PLACE top crust over filling and trim to fit pie plate. Cut a few vents in top crust. Seal bottom and top crusts together firmly.

BAKE on lower rack of oven for 15 minutes. Reduce heat to 375 F and bake for 30 minutes longer, or until pastry is golden brown and filling is bubbling.

Caramelized Lemon Tartlets

SERVES 4

Make life easy and use storebought tart shells and lemon curd. Or combine 1 cup short-bread cookie crumbs with ¼ cup melted butter. Pat into tart pans lined with plastic wrap and chill (do not bake).

4 baked tart shells

1 cup lemon curd or lemon cream (page 264)

1 tbsp granulated sugar

3 golden or green kiwis, sliced

FILL tart shells with lemon curd, spreading curd right across top of pastry to help prevent burning. Chill for 1 hour.

PREHEAT broiler.

SIFT sugar evenly over tart shells. Place tarts under broiler. Watch carefully and broil just until sugar turns golden. Chill.

SERVE tarts with sliced kiwi.

Cinnamon Plum Tart

SERVES 6

This is a Scottish favourite. It is like a plum quiche with a crunchy cinnamon topping. If you use the small blue plums, increase the number to twelve. Use a sweet pastry pie crust (page 237), baked blind (or you could buy a prebaked tart shell).

8 plums, pitted and quartered
1 partially baked 9-inch pie crust
1 cup whipping cream
3 eggs

3 tbsp lemon juice
$\frac{1}{2}$ cup granulated sugar
2 tsp ground cinnamon
3 tbsp brown sugar

PREHEAT oven to 350 F.

ARRANGE plums in pie crust, skin side up.

WHISK cream, eggs, lemon juice, granulated sugar and 1 tsp cinnamon in a bowl. Pour mixture over plums.

BAKE for 25 minutes, or until plums are softened.

COMBINE brown sugar and remaining 1 tsp cinnamon in a small bowl. Sprinkle over tart. Bake for 10 to 15 minutes longer, or until tart is puffed and crusty. Serve warm or at room temperature.

Cherry Strudel

To pit the cherries, just squeeze the pits out with your fingers. Sour cherries are also available frozen and pitted. Drain them well after defrosting.

Filling

1 lb (500 g) sour cherries, pitted

$1/2$ cup ground almonds

$1/2$ cup granulated sugar

$1/4$ cup fresh breadcrumbs

$1/4$ tsp ground cinnamon

Pastry

8 sheets phyllo pastry, defrosted

$1/4$ cup granulated sugar

$1/4$ cup ground almonds

$1/2$ cup butter, melted

PREHEAT oven to 375 F.

COMBINE cherries, almonds, sugar, breadcrumbs and cinnamon in a bowl. Reserve.

PREPARE pastry by placing stack of phyllo on counter. Cover with a tea towel. Combine sugar and almonds in a small bowl.

BRUSH one sheet of phyllo with a little melted butter using a pastry brush. Sprinkle about 1 tbsp almond mixture over butter. Top with second sheet, brush with a little butter and sprinkle with almond mixture. Repeat with remaining sheets of phyllo.

SPREAD cherry filling over phyllo, leaving about 2 inches clear along long sides and 1 inch clear along short sides. Fold in short sides and roll phyllo lengthwise into a strudel shape. Place on a greased baking sheet. Brush with remaining butter and cut 3 slits in top.

BAKE for 20 to 25 minutes, or until top is browned.

Blueberry Lime Loaf

MAKES 1 LOAF

This is my favourite easy cake for nibbling. It's the beat-everything-in-one-bowl method. Use any fruit except strawberries or raspberries, which are too soft. Serve the cake on its own as a snack or with ice cream and extra fruit for dessert.

1/2 cup butter, softened	1 tsp baking powder
1 cup granulated sugar	1/2 tsp salt
2 eggs	1 cup blueberries, chopped plums or chopped
1/4 cup sour cream	apricots
1 tbsp grated lime rind	2 tbsp lime juice
1 1/2 cups all-purpose flour	2 tbsp icing sugar

PREHEAT oven to 350 F. Line bottom of a loaf pan with parchment paper. Butter sides and sprinkle with a little sugar.

BEAT butter (butter should be very soft) and granulated sugar in a large bowl with an electric mixer until combined. Beat in eggs, sour cream and lime rind.

SIFT flour, baking powder and salt into batter and beat with an electric mixer for 3 minutes, or until mixture is smooth and some air has been incorporated. Stir in blueberries. Spoon batter into loaf pan (batter will be quite thick).

BAKE for 45 to 55 minutes, or until top is golden and a cake tester comes out clean.

WHISK lime juice and icing sugar in a bowl. Poke holes through warm cake with a skewer. Brush cake with lime syrup while cake is still in pan. Cool slightly before unmoulding.

{ measuring and sifting flour }

Most flour is presifted. But sifting is still the best way to combine the flour with other ingredients.

Measure the flour before sifting by scooping the flour loosely into a dry measuring cup. Do not tap the cup. Draw a knife across top of the measuring cup to sweep off the excess flour. Place the flour in a sieve and shake into a bowl or onto a piece of wax paper.

Peaches and Pound Cake with Crème Fraîche

SERVES 6

Another favourite with *Globe and Mail* readers. Use 2 cups fresh berries instead of the peaches if desired.

4 peaches, peeled and sliced
2 tbsp granulated sugar
2 tbsp lemon juice

Cake
1 1/2 cups all-purpose flour
1 tsp baking powder

1/2 tsp salt
1 tbsp grated lemon rind
1/2 cup butter, at room temperature
1 cup granulated sugar
2 eggs
1/2 cup buttermilk
1 cup crème fraîche or whipped cream

PREHEAT oven to 350 F. Line bottom of a loaf pan with parchment paper. Butter sides and sprinkle with a little sugar.

PLACE peaches in a bowl and sprinkle with sugar and lemon juice. Reserve.

SIFT flour, baking powder and salt into a bowl. Stir in lemon rind.

BEAT butter and sugar in a large bowl with an electric mixer until light and fluffy. Beat in eggs one at a time.

BEAT in one-third of flour mixture. Beat in 1/4 cup buttermilk. Repeat, beating well after each addition and finishing with flour mixture.

POUR batter into loaf pan and bake for 55 minutes, or until a cake tester comes out clean.

POKE holes through warm cake with a skewer. While cake is still in pan, brush with peach juice that has collected in bowl. Cool.

SLICE cake and top with peaches and crème fraîche.

{ crème fraîche }

Combine 2 tbsp buttermilk and 1 cup whipping cream in a glass jar. Leave on counter in a warm place, shaking jar occasionally, for 24 hours, or until thickened. Refrigerate for up to 2 weeks.

Makes about 1 cup.

The most important step in making a cake is the proper creaming of the butter and sugar.

Use an electric mixer or hand mixer. Allow the butter to come to room temperature before starting, or process it in a food processor for 3 to 5 seconds. Never melt it to soften; this will change the texture of the butter so air cannot be beaten into it successfully.

Beat the butter until it is light, soft and airy. Add the sugar a few spoonfuls at a time and beat after each addition until the mixture is very light and fluffy and no grains of sugar are visible.

Add the eggs one at a time and beat each in thoroughly before adding the next. If the butter and egg mixture curdles (starts to separate), the butter and sugar were not creamed well enough. Beat in a little flour to bring it together again.

Add the dry and liquid ingredients to the butter and egg mixture, alternating, and making three flour mixture additions and two liquid additions. After each addition, stir to combine, beat well for a few seconds, then scrape down the sides of the bowl and beaters with a spatula.

For one-bowl cakes, which are usually very simple, all the ingredients should be at room temperature. Using an electric mixer, beat all the ingredients together like mad for 3 minutes, or until the batter is soft and well combined.

Pour or spoon the batter into the prepared cake pan, then smooth evenly with a spatula.

Cakes should be baked on the middle rack of the oven. If you are using more than one rack, switch the position of the pans halfway through the baking time.

A cake is done when the edges have pulled away slightly from the sides of the pan, and the top of the cake springs back lightly when touched, or when a toothpick inserted in the centre of the cake comes out clean.

Cool cakes on a wire rack in the cake pan for 10 minutes. Slide a spatula around the sides, then invert onto a wire rack to cool completely. Cakes are best eaten within one or two days.

Classic Chocolate Cake

SERVES 8

This is an easy traditional chocolate cake with lots of flavour and a moist texture. My daughter Katie once baked it in a stainless-steel bowl to make a ladybug cake for her own daughter.

$\frac{1}{2}$ cup butter, at room temperature

1 cup granulated sugar

2 eggs

1 $\frac{1}{2}$ cups all-purpose flour

$\frac{1}{4}$ cup cocoa powder

1 tsp baking soda

$\frac{1}{2}$ tsp salt

1 cup buttermilk

1 tsp vanilla

4 oz (125 g) bittersweet chocolate, melted and
    cooled to room temperature

Chocolate Filling

6 oz (175 g) bittersweet chocolate, chopped

$\frac{1}{4}$ cup butter, at room temperature

$\frac{1}{3}$ cup deli-style cream cheese

2 tbsp orange liqueur or Kahlua, optional

Chocolate Butter Glaze

4 oz (125 g) bittersweet chocolate, chopped

$\frac{1}{4}$ cup butter

1 tsp corn syrup

PREHEAT oven to 325 F. Line bottom of a 9-inch springform pan with parchment paper. Butter sides of pan and dust with flour.

COMBINE butter and sugar in a large bowl. Beat with an electric mixer until light and fluffy. Add eggs one at a time, beating well after each addition.

SIFT flour, cocoa, baking soda and salt into a bowl. Add sifted ingredients to butter-sugar mixture, alternating with buttermilk, and blending lightly between additions. Beat in vanilla and melted chocolate until batter is a uniform colour.

SPOON batter into prepared pan and bake for 55 minutes, or until cake is firm to touch and a tester comes out clean.

PREPARE filling while cake is baking. Melt chocolate in a heavy pot over low heat. Stir in butter, cream cheese and liqueur. Remove pot from heat and let cool for 20 minutes, or until spreadable.

TRIM top of cake so it is flat and smooth. Slice cake in half horizontally with a large serrated knife. Spread bottom half of cake with filling and place top half over filling.

PREPARE glaze by combining chocolate, butter and corn syrup in a heavy pot over low heat. Stir until melted. Pour glaze over top of cake, letting it drip down sides.

Marmalade Cake

SERVES 6

Marmalade cake has always been my favourite, probably because of my Scottish upbringing.
Having made several recipes over the past few years, this one is my current choice. It is
made in one bowl. Throw everything in and beat it together, but the butter must be very
soft, otherwise it won't come together. It is a thick batter.

½ cup butter, softened	**Glaze**
1 cup granulated sugar	½ cup granulated sugar
2 eggs	¼ cup orange juice
¼ cup Seville orange marmalade	
1 tsp grated orange rind	
1 ½ cups all-purpose flour	
1 ½ tsp baking powder	
½ tsp salt	

PREHEAT oven to 350 F. Line bottom of an 8-inch round cake pan with parchment paper.
Butter sides of pan.

BEAT butter and sugar in a large bowl with an electric mixer. Beat in eggs, marmalade and
orange rind.

SIFT flour, baking powder and salt into batter. Beat with an electric mixer until well combined, about 3 minutes. Spoon batter into prepared cake pan.

BAKE for 45 to 50 minutes, or until a cake tester comes out clean. Place a piece of parchment paper over top of the cake during the final 15 minutes of baking to keep it from
becoming too brown.

COMBINE sugar and orange juice in a small pot and bring to a boil. Remove from heat.
Prick holes in warm cake and brush with several coats of glaze.

REMOVE cake from pan, peel off paper and set on a rack over a plate.

{ baking powder }

Baking powder goes stale over time. To test it for freshness, combine 1 tsp
baking powder with ⅓ cup hot water. If the baking powder is fresh, it will rapidly fizz and
bubble.

{ desserts }

Frozen Chocolate Loaf

SERVES 8 TO 10

This sensational dessert stays in the freezer until you need it. Use the best chocolate you can buy. The darker and deeper the flavour, the better.

8 oz (250 g) bittersweet chocolate, coarsely
    chopped
1 cup butter, cubed
$\frac{1}{3}$ cup water
4 eggs
1 cup granulated sugar
1 tbsp all-purpose flour

Garnish
1 cup lightly whipped cream
Fresh raspberries or other fruit in season

PREHEAT oven to 350 F. Butter a loaf pan and line base and sides with parchment paper.

COMBINE chocolate, butter and water in a heavy pot over low heat and stir until melted. Cool slightly.

BEAT eggs and sugar in a large bowl with an electric mixer until light and fluffy. Beat in flour. Gradually beat in chocolate mixture. Pour into loaf pan.

PLACE loaf pan in a roasting pan and pour boiling water into roasting pan until water reaches halfway up sides of loaf pan. Bake for 1 hour, or until firm on top and a cake tester comes out clean. Remove from oven, cool and refrigerate in loaf pan until really set.

TURN out onto a large sheet of parchment paper. Fold paper over chocolate loaf, wrap in foil and freeze.

REMOVE cake from freezer about 15 minutes before cutting. Cut into slices and serve with cream and raspberries.

We now know that dark chocolate is actually good for you. It provides antioxidants that protect against nasty diseases, and it even contains healthy fibre. But it isn't enough anymore just to call it chocolate. Chocolate has become as rarified as single malt whisky—each with its own history, country of origin and type of bean.

Like tea, coffee and wine, chocolate varies depending on the conditions in which the beans are grown. Chocolate from Madagascar, for instance, is highly aromatic, with notes of vanilla, caramel and gingerbread, while Santo Domingo chocolate is fruity, with a hint of green olives.

The percentage shown on the label tells you the amount of cocoa solids in the chocolate. For example, 70 percent bittersweet chocolate means that 70 percent is pure chocolate liquor, and the remainder is made up of cocoa butter, sugar, lecithin and sometimes vanilla. I like to use 70 percent chocolate in chocolate mousse and other really chocolaty desserts; 60 to 65 percent is fine for all other baking. (I recommend French, Swiss or Belgian chocolate, or the American Scharffen Berger.)

White chocolate is not really chocolate at all, as it does not contain chocolate liquor. It is a mix of sugar, vanilla, cocoa butter and milk solids. Check the ingredient list; white chocolate that contains vegetable shortening instead of cocoa butter is bland and boring.

Chocolate Mousse with Saffron Foam

SERVES 6

This is the ultimate chocolate mousse. It's a takeoff on a chocolate dessert I had in Paris that was served with saffron foam. The saffron highlights the chocolate and adds a beautiful colour, but you could also serve the mousse with whipped cream.

8 oz (250 g) bittersweet chocolate, chopped	**Saffron Foam**
1 cup whipping cream	Pinch saffron threads
3 eggs	1/2 cup whipping cream
1/4 cup granulated sugar	2 tbsp granulated sugar

HEAT chocolate and cream in a heavy pot over low heat, stirring until chocolate melts and mixture is smooth. Remove from heat.

COMBINE eggs and sugar in a metal bowl over simmering water (basically a big homemade double boiler) and beat with an electric mixer for 5 minutes, or until mixture is pale yellow and when you lift beaters, mixture forms a ribbon that takes 5 seconds to dissipate. Remove bowl from heat.

FOLD chocolate mixture into egg mixture. Mixture will be quite runny. Refrigerate for 4 hours or overnight. Mousse will thicken.

PREPARE saffron foam by heating saffron and 2 tbsp whipping cream in a small pot over low heat until cream is an orangey colour. Combine saffron cream with remaining cream and sugar. Beat until slightly airy and thick enough to coat a spoon.

SCOOP mousse onto a plate or glass serving dish and surround with foam.

Brownie Pudding

SERVES 6

My friend Nancy Usher has been making this pudding for her kids for years, and now her grandchildren demand it. It is a little crumbly, slightly saucy and utterly decadent. Serve it warm with ice cream.

1 cup all-purpose flour	2 eggs
2/3 cup cocoa powder	1 cup granulated sugar
1 tsp baking powder	1/2 cup milk
1/2 tsp salt	1 tsp vanilla
6 tbsp butter	1/2 cup brown sugar
1/2 cup chopped bittersweet chocolate	1 1/3 cups boiling water

PREHEAT oven to 350 F.

SIFT flour, 1/3 cup cocoa, baking powder and salt into a bowl.

MELT butter and chocolate in a small heavy pot over low heat. Remove from heat and cool slightly.

WHISK eggs, granulated sugar, milk and vanilla in a bowl until well combined. Add melted chocolate mixture and flour mixture and stir until batter is just combined.

SPREAD batter evenly in a greased 8-inch square baking pan.

WHISK remaining 1/3 cocoa powder, brown sugar and boiling water in a bowl. Pour mixture over batter.

BAKE for 35 to 40 minutes, or until a tester comes out clean but cake still has a little wiggle. Do not overbake.

Blueberry Brittle with White Chocolate Ice Cream

SERVES 4

A deluxe blueberry crisp with an especially crunchy topping. It is even better made with tiny wild blueberries (if you use frozen berries, use them in their frozen state).

3 cups blueberries

1/4 cup granulated sugar

1 tsp grated lemon rind

3/4 cup all-purpose flour

1/2 cup Demerara sugar

1/2 tsp ground cinnamon

Pinch salt

1/4 cup butter, cubed

2 cups white chocolate ice cream

PREHEAT oven to 350 F.

COMBINE blueberries, granulated sugar and lemon rind in a bowl. Spread in a buttered baking dish.

COMBINE flour, Demerara sugar, cinnamon and salt in a food processor. Sprinkle butter over mixture and process until mixture resembles coarse breadcrumbs. Sprinkle over fruit.

BAKE for 35 to 40 minutes, or until golden brown. Serve with white chocolate ice cream.

{ white chocolate ice cream }

Melt 1 cup white chocolate with 1/4 cup whipping cream in a heavy pot or a double boiler over low heat. Remove from heat when chocolate is barely melted. Cool slightly. Gradually (or the chocolate may seize) stir in 2 cups softened vanilla ice cream. Pack into a freezer container and freeze for at least 2 hours. (If mixture does seize, just cut up the chocolate and call it white chocolate chunk ice cream.)

Makes about 2 cups.

Fruit Salad with Lemongrass and Ginger Syrup

SERVES 4

Have some lichee liqueur left over from that martini party? Turn it into a fragrant sugar syrup that flavours fruit beautifully. Use any fresh fruit in season. Reserve a little of the syrup and beat it into whipping cream to serve with the fruit salad.

1 stalk lemongrass

2 tbsp chopped pickled ginger

1/2 cup brown sugar

1/2 cup water

1 tsp grated lemon rind

2 tbsp lemon juice

1/4 cup lichee or other fruit liqueur

2 cups sliced strawberries

2 cups blueberries

2 cups raspberries

1 cup red or black currants

Fresh lemon balm or mint sprigs

CUT lemongrass into 2-inch pieces and smash with base of a pot to bruise it. Place in a pot and add ginger, sugar, water, lemon rind and juice. Bring to a boil, reduce heat and simmer for 5 minutes. Cool and strain. Stir in lichee liqueur.

LAYER fruit in a glass bowl. Pour syrup over fruit. Garnish with lemon balm.

Lemon Panna Cotta

SERVES 4

A light dessert that is perfect after a large meal. Panna cotta is basically a smooth custard set with gelatine instead of eggs. The size of your ramekins will determine how many you can make. I like to use 1-cup ramekins but not everyone has them. I have also used espresso cups or small tea cups. Served with a stunning blackberry sauce, this looks as beautiful as it tastes.

1 cup milk	⅓ cup granulated sugar
1 tbsp powdered gelatine	2 tsp grated lemon rind
2 cups whipping cream	

HEAT ¼ cup milk in a small pot over low heat. Sprinkle gelatine over milk. Dissolve slowly, stirring occasionally. Reserve. (If gelatine becomes solid again before using, reheat to liquefy.)

COMBINE remaining milk, cream, sugar and lemon rind in a pot. Bring to a boil, reduce heat and simmer for 5 minutes. Remove from heat and stir in gelatine mixture. Cool, stirring occasionally, until room temperature.

STRAIN custard into four oiled 1-cup ramekins. Refrigerate for 4 hours, or until set. Turn out onto individual serving dishes.

{ blackberry sauce }

Combine ½ cup fresh or frozen blackberries with 2 tbsp granulated sugar and 2 tbsp Port in a small pot. Bring to a boil and boil for 3 to 5 minutes, or until blackberries have broken down and sauce is thick. Add another ½ cup whole blackberries and ½ tsp grated lemon rind.

Makes about ¾ cup.

{ gelatine }

Gelatine is a substance made from animal bones, and it helps set certain desserts, fruit purees and pâtés. Each envelope of powdered gelatine contains a tablespoon, and it is mixed with a little water and warmed before being stirred into the remaining ingredients.

There is a vegetarian version called agar-agar, which can be found at health food stores. To use, follow the package directions.

Raspberry Parfait with Oatmeal and Scotch

SERVES 4

I like easy desserts that don't take long to prepare. Here's one of my favourites. It is an easy Scottish dessert that is very pretty and a little unusual, with a rich, complex taste. Make it in parfait glasses and top with whipped cream and raspberries.

1 cup whipping cream	1 tbsp granulated sugar
½ cup deli-style cream cheese	1 ½ cups raspberries
2 tbsp honey	1 cup crumbled oatmeal cookies
⅓ cup single malt whisky	

WHIP cream in a bowl until soft peaks form.

COMBINE cream cheese, honey, whisky and sugar in a large bowl and blend until smooth. Taste and add sugar if desired. Fold in whipped cream.

LAYER 2 tbsp raspberries in bottom of each of four glasses. Top with some of the cream mixture and sprinkle with cookies. Repeat layers. Garnish top of each parfait with a raspberry.

{ sugar }

Sugar is primarily used as a sweetener. However, it also gives baked goods colour as it caramelizes in the oven, and it helps them retain moisture and acts as a preservative, allowing them to stay fresh longer. Finally, sugar adds leavening by allowing greater expansion of trapped air.

The granulated sugar we use most is made from sugar cane and has been refined to make it white.

Brown sugar is unrefined; it adds a butterscotch flavour and chewier texture to baked goods, as well as darkening the colour. But not all brown sugar is created equal. Some are refined white sugar with molasses added. Check the label to make sure you are getting the real deal. (To stop regular brown sugar from hardening, keep it in an airtight container or put a strip of apple peel in the bag.)

Demerara is a coarse-grained unrefined brown sugar that adds an extra crunch to desserts. It is wonderful in coffee and for baking, especially when you want crunch, and it never seems to harden the way other brown sugars do.

Icing or confectioner's sugar is finely ground sugar that dissolves instantly. Use it in icings.

Peach and Blueberry Cobbler

SERVES 6

This is a much-requested recipe. The cornmeal gives this topping an unusual crunch. Any leftovers are wonderful for breakfast the next day. This can also be made with other fruit, such as pears, apricots, plums or raspberries.

4 cups peeled and sliced peaches	**Topping**
1 cup blueberries	1/2 cup all-purpose flour
2 tbsp lemon juice	1/2 cup cornmeal
2 tbsp brown sugar	1/4 cup brown sugar
1 tbsp cornstarch	1/4 tsp ground nutmeg
1 tbsp butter	1/4 cup butter, cubed
	1/2 cup whipping cream

PREHEAT oven to 350 F.

COMBINE peaches, blueberries, lemon juice, sugar and cornstarch in a large bowl. Spread fruit in a buttered baking dish and dot with butter.

PREPARE topping by combining flour, cornmeal, sugar and nutmeg in a bowl. Cut in butter until mixture is crumbly.

STIR in cream until mixture is just moistened. Drop batter by heaping spoonfuls onto fruit mixture. Topping will spread slightly during baking.

BAKE for 30 to 35 minutes, or until topping is browned and fruit is bubbling. Serve warm.

Figs Baked in Wine

SERVES 4

This is the simplest recipe that I've made lately. I had some late harvest Riesling left over (you need a sweet wine for this dessert), poured it over some figs and baked it. It turned into a lovely fragrant concoction perfect for serving with ice cream or frozen yogurt.

12 fresh figs   1/2 cup late harvest Riesling

PREHEAT oven to 400 F.

CUT figs in half and place flesh side down in a baking dish. Pour wine over top.

BAKE for 20 minutes, or until figs are softened and wine has reduced to a syrup.

Lemon Cream

SERVES 4

This simple lemon cream packs lots of flavour. It is based on a recipe from my friend Annabel Langbein, a New Zealand cookbook author who made it for us at her home in Wanaka, the most beautiful part of the South Island. Serve with a cookie. (I also sometimes use it instead of lemon curd as a tart filling.)

1 cup whipping cream   1 tsp grated lemon rind
1/2 cup granulated sugar   1/4 cup lemon juice
1/4 cup butter

COMBINE cream, sugar and butter in a small pot and bring to a boil, stirring constantly. Reduce heat and simmer, stirring occasionally, for 3 minutes. Remove from heat.

STIR in lemon rind and juice. Pour mixture into four 1-cup ramekins and chill until set, about 2 hours.

Roasted Apples with Caramel Sauce

SERVES 6

Another very easy dessert. Serve the apples topped with a scoop of ice cream. Use a tart apple such as Spy, Mutsu or Ida Red, rather than the softer McIntosh or Red Delicious, which fall to mush when cooked.

6 tart apples, peeled and quartered
$\frac{1}{2}$ cup brown sugar
1 tbsp all-purpose flour
1 tsp ground cinnamon

$\frac{1}{4}$ cup butter, melted
$\frac{1}{2}$ cup apple juice
1 tbsp chopped crystallized ginger

PREHEAT oven to 375 F.

PLACE apples, cored side up, in a buttered baking dish.

COMBINE sugar, flour and cinnamon in a bowl. Stir in melted butter, apple juice and ginger. Pour mixture over apples. Cover with foil and bake for 20 minutes.

UNCOVER and bake for 15 minutes longer. Serve warm with juices.

Plum and Shortbread Swirls

SERVES 6

A quick, beautiful dessert that can be served layered in wine glasses. If you make this with the smaller blue or prune plums, use eighteen.

9 plums, halved	1 cup whipping cream
³⁄₄ cup orange juice	1 cup mascarpone
2 tbsp granulated sugar	¹⁄₂ cup plain yogurt
1 ¹⁄₂ cups broken shortbread cookies	2 tbsp maple syrup
¹⁄₃ cup orange liqueur	1 tsp grated orange rind

PREHEAT oven to 350 F.

PLACE plums, cut side up, in a baking dish. Pour orange juice over top and sprinkle with sugar. Bake for 25 minutes, or until soft and very juicy. Cool in juices.

CUT plums into quarters. Reserve plums and juices together.

COMBINE cookie pieces and orange liqueur in a bowl.

WHIP cream in a large bowl until it holds soft peaks.

COMBINE mascarpone, yogurt, maple syrup and orange rind in a bowl. Fold in whipped cream.

LAYER mascarpone mixture, cookies, plums and any juices in two layers in 6 wine glasses or small glass dishes, ending with a dollop of mascarpone.

{ mascarpone }

A buttery, rich Italian cream cheese with a velvety texture that can be used in desserts and sauces. Substitute soft deli-style cream cheese if necessary.

Strawberries with Tarragon Syrup

SERVES 4

The slightly licorice flavour of the tarragon adds a mysterious quality to this lovely, quick dessert. You can use fresh rosemary or lavender as a tarragon substitute. If you don't mind the green flecks, don't bother straining the syrup. It keeps 2 or 3 days.

1 cup water	4 cups sliced strawberries
1 cup granulated sugar	2 cups vanilla ice cream
2 tbsp finely chopped fresh tarragon	Fresh tarragon sprigs

BRING water, sugar and chopped tarragon to a boil in a pot. Boil for 2 minutes. Cool.

STRAIN syrup over sliced strawberries and marinate for about 1 hour.

SERVE strawberries over ice cream, garnished with a sprig of tarragon.

Roasted Fruit

SERVES 8

Roasting fruit brings out the natural sugars. This is especially good made with slightly underripe fruit. Use any combination of peaches, plums, apricots or nectarines. Serve it with ice cream, drizzled with the pan juices.

2 lb (1 kg) peaches, plums, apricots or nectarines
$1/2$ cup brown sugar
2 tbsp lemon juice

PREHEAT oven to 350 F.

CUT fruit in half and remove pits but do not peel. Place cut side up in a baking dish.

SPRINKLE fruit with sugar and lemon juice. Bake for 20 to 25 minutes, depending on ripeness, or until tender. Stir fruit occasionally.

CHILL before serving.

Instant Cherry Meringues

SERVES 4

A quick and easy dessert; buy the prebaked meringues at the supermarket. Cherry pitters make quick work of pitting, or cut the cherries in half to remove the pits.

½ cup granulated sugar

1 cup water

3 cups pitted Bing or Rainier cherries

1 tsp cornstarch

1 tbsp water

4 prebaked meringues (about 4 inches
   in diameter)

2 cups vanilla ice cream

BRING sugar and 1 cup water to a boil in a pot and boil for 2 minutes. Add 1½ cups cherries and simmer for 10 minutes, or until soft.

TRANSFER liquid and cooked cherries to a food processor and puree until smooth. Return puree to pot.

COMBINE cornstarch and 1 tbsp water in a cup until smooth. Stir into puree and bring to a boil, stirring. Remove from heat and stir in remaining uncooked cherries.

TOP each meringue with ½ cup ice cream. Pour cherry sauce over and around meringues.

{ cherries }

My favourite cherries for eating are Rainier—blushing pink and white

cherries that are slightly less sweet than the fat, dark-red Bing cherries. Tart red sour cherries are good for pies and baking, and are often available frozen.

Lemongrass Pots de Crème with Berries

SERVES 6

These delicate, fabulous custards are made in espresso cups, baked in a water bath (page 30) and topped with mixed fresh berries. Use any kind of fruit to top them or just whip some cream. Most espresso cups can go in the oven as the heat is very gentle.

3 stalks lemongrass	5 egg yolks
1/2 cup whipping cream	1/3 cup granulated sugar
2 cups whole milk	1 1/2 cups fresh berries
1 tsp vanilla	

CUT off all but bottom 4 inches of lemongrass, reserving tops for another purpose. Use back of a knife or pot to smash lemongrass stalk to release juices. Chop stalk coarsely.

COMBINE cream, milk and lemongrass in a small pot. Bring to a boil over medium heat. Remove from heat and let sit for 30 minutes.

PREHEAT oven to 300 F.

STRAIN out lemongrass and return milk mixture to pot. Bring to a boil and remove from heat. Stir in vanilla.

BEAT egg yolks in a bowl. Whisk in sugar and warm cream mixture. Strain into a measuring cup.

PLACE six ramekins or ovenproof espresso cups in a large roasting pan. Pour custard into ramekins until three-quarters full. Pour boiling water into roasting pan until water comes halfway up sides of ramekins. Place a sheet of parchment paper over ramekins.

BAKE for 30 minutes, or until custards have a slight wobble in the centre. Remove ramekins from water bath and cool. Serve with berries piled on top.

Winter Apple Pudding

SERVES 6

Steamed puddings have fallen out of fashion, but everyone loves this apple-based dessert. It is oven-steamed, making it easier, lighter and quicker than most steamed puddings. Serve it after Christmas dinner—or any time—with extra caramel sauce and custard or plain old ice cream.

Caramel

$1/2$ cup granulated sugar

$1/4$ cup water

1 tbsp corn syrup

Pudding

$1/2$ cup butter, at room temperature

$1/2$ cup brown sugar

3 eggs

$1/2$ cup dried cranberries

$1/2$ cup coarsely chopped pecans

2 tart apples, peeled and chopped

2 tsp grated orange rind

$1/4$ cup orange juice

$1/2$ cup apple cider

$1/4$ cup all-purpose flour

$1 1/2$ cups fresh breadcrumbs

1 tsp ground cinnamon

Pinch salt

PREHEAT oven to 350 F.

COMBINE granulated sugar, water and corn syrup in a heavy pot over medium heat. Heat until sugar has melted. Bring to a boil and boil for 5 to 7 minutes, or until caramel turns golden. Pour into a buttered 6-cup stainless-steel or ovenproof bowl, swirling to coat bowl with caramel. Reserve.

CREAM butter and brown sugar in a large bowl until light and fluffy. Beat in eggs one at a time. Stir in cranberries, pecans, apples, orange rind, orange juice and apple cider.

COMBINE flour, breadcrumbs, cinnamon and salt in a separate bowl. Stir half the flour mixture into apple mixture until well blended, then blend in remaining flour mixture.

TURN batter into caramel-lined bowl and cover with foil. Place in a deep roasting pan. Pour boiling water into pan until it reaches halfway up sides of bowl. Bake in centre of oven for 45 minutes. Remove foil and bake for 45 minutes longer, or until a cake tester comes out clean. Let cool slightly and turn out onto a serving plate. Serve warm or cold.

Fig and Mascarpone Trifle

SERVES 4

Figs always make a sensual dessert, and this one takes no time to make. Serve it in glass tumblers for a fashionable look. You could use deli-style cream cheese instead of the mascarpone.

8 fresh figs, halved or quartered if large	1 cup mascarpone
1/2 cup cranberry juice	1/4 cup sour cream
1/2 cup Port	1 tbsp granulated sugar
2 cups crumbled biscotti (about 2 biscuits)	1/4 cup whipping cream

PREHEAT oven to 400 F.

PLACE figs in a baking dish. Combine cranberry juice and Port and toss with figs. Roast for 10 minutes, or until figs are soft.

POUR liquid from baking dish into a small pot. Bring to a boil and cook for about 6 minutes, or until slightly syrupy. Stir biscotti into syrup.

COMBINE mascarpone, sour cream and sugar in a large bowl.

BEAT whipping cream in a separate bowl with an electric mixer until soft peaks form. Fold into mascarpone mixture.

PLACE a spoonful of biscotti in bottom of individual glass dishes or cups. Top with some figs and mascarpone. Repeat layers, finishing with a dab of mascarpone cream.

Creamy Rice Pudding with Cranberries

SERVES 4 TO 6

This is inspired by my grandmother's rice pudding, although she did not use arborio rice, as it was unavailable in Scotland at that time. Arborio gives this an extra-creamy texture, as it absorbs the liquid so well. Use raisins instead of cranberries or omit the fruit altogether if desired.

5 cups milk

½ cup granulated sugar

½ cup arborio rice

1 tsp grated orange rind

Pinch salt

½ cup dried cranberries

1 tsp vanilla

2 tbsp butter

½ cup whipping cream

¼ tsp ground cinnamon, or to taste

BRING milk, sugar, rice, orange rind and salt to a boil in a pot over high heat. Reduce heat and simmer, stirring occasionally, for 35 minutes.

ADD cranberries and cook for 15 minutes, or until rice is tender and liquid has been absorbed. Rice should be very creamy.

STIR in vanilla and simmer for 2 minutes. Stir in butter.

POUR pudding into a buttered bowl and cover with plastic wrap. Cool.

WHIP cream in a bowl until soft peaks form. Fold into cooled pudding. Sprinkle with cinnamon.

{ acknowledgements }

This is the most personal book I have written, and it is through the help and dedication of my family, friends and coworkers that it is here at all.

Eshun Mott is my recipe tester, associate and alter ego. She loves to bake, is totally accurate and makes sure everything works to perfection.

I cannot work without my editor Shelley Tanaka, who makes it all read so beautifully. When a book is finished, I always look at it in admiration, wondering how I could have produced it. Without Shelley, I am not sure I could.

Photographer Rob Fiocca took on a challenge by shooting the whole book in my kitchen over three days with the help of Jim Norton, who produced the stunning chapter openers. (It was quite the Hollywood scene in my kitchen with two photographers, three photo assistants, my two cooking assistants, the book designer and editor, computers and lights.)

At Random House, Tanya Trafford and Kendall Anderson shepherded the book with style and gave me good insights. Anne Collins, my publisher, was wonderful, warm and unflappable. The talented Kelly Hill created a superb design and was always willing to listen and help.

Bruce Westwood, who loves good food almost as much as I do, is an agent *par excellence*. He fought the battles, leaving me to reap the benefits.

My colleagues Domini Clarke and Sheree Lee Olsen at the *Globe and Mail* and Jody Dunn and Vivianna Kouwenhoven at *Food & Drink* have always encouraged me, and I'm grateful for their ongoing support.

My family is a large part of everything I do. My dear husband and partner, Bruce, is always supportive and helps me be a better person. And Emma, Micah, Katie, Shane, Alex and Nat put up with my long working hours, which means I do not have as much time for my grandchildren as I would like.

And my appreciation goes to my wonderful women friends who cook for me, listen to me and help to keep me sane.

Finally, it was my late mother, Pearl Geneen, who instilled in me the love of good food and the desire to inspire others.

{ culinary skills }

{ ingredient information }

{ the author }

Lucy Waverman is a Cordon Bleu–trained chef and the author of eight cookbooks, including the award-winning *Dinner Tonight* and *Home for Dinner*. She has a weekly column in the *Globe and Mail* and is Food Editor at *Food & Drink* magazine. Lucy was a culinary expert on CityLine for twelve years. Her most recent book, A *Matter of Taste* (with James Chatto), was a finalist for a James Beard Entertaining Award and won the Gold Medal at Cuisine Canada's 2005 culinary cookbook awards. She lives in Toronto with her husband.

Please visit Lucy Waverman's website at www.lucywaverman.com

{ the photographer }

Rob Fiocca has earned a reputation as one of North America's most sought-after food, product and interior photographers. Throughout his career he has won several photographic awards including a Cordon d'or gold ribbon and many National Magazine Awards. When not in his Toronto studio, Rob is accepting new challenges across the continent, often in San Francisco, L.A., New York and Chicago and Miami.